W9-BEA-886

Praise for
The ABCs of Choosing a Good Wife

"The writer of Proverbs poses the question, 'An excellent wife, who can find?' The answer is, 'You—if you know what you're looking for.' Steve Wood offers invaluable insight into choosing a good wife; if acted upon, his suggestions may change your life and the lives of others for eternity. The destiny of your future children may very well come down to one choice. Make it a good one! Not only is [this book] a tremendous resource for choosing your lifelong marriage partner—it is a fabulous devotional for fathers in training their sons."

> **—Jeff Cavins, Executive Director of**
> **Programming and Production,**
> **Starboard Network**

"It might seem like an impossible task, but this book shows that you can do it. Not only that, you can keep your faith, your integrity, and your joy through the whole process of discerning God's will, finding Miss Right, and entering the marriage covenant. Steve Wood reviews and evaluates many of the current debates about dating and courtship. Parents need this book. So do their children. And so do men who have been looking for a long time and who have grown weary of the dating culture."

> **—Scott Hahn, Ph.D., founder**
> **St. Paul Center for Biblical Theology**

"*The ABCs of Choosing a Good Wife* is the BEST marriage preparation book ever written for men. It will help men accomplish one of their most important missions in life: choosing a good wife. I am buying copies for my son and my nephews."

> **—Hugh Williamson, major, USMCR**
> **Federal law enforcement agent**

The ABCs of Choosing a Good Wife

The ABCs of Choosing a Good Wife

Stephen Wood

Family Life Center Publications

Copyright © 2003 Family Life Center Publications
All rights reserved. No part of this book may be reproduced or transmit-
ted in any form or by any means, electronic or mechanical, including
photocopying, recording or by any information storage or retrieval
system, without permission in writing from the publisher.

ISBN: 0-972757-10-4
Library of Congress Catalog Card Number: 2003100171
Book production and design: Tabby House
Cover design: Catherine Wood
Manufactured in the United States of America

Unless otherwise indicated, Scripture quotations are taken from the
Revised Standard Version, Catholic Edition [RSVCE], copyright © 1965
and 1966 by the Division of Christian Education of the National
Council of the Churches of Christ in the United States of America.
Used by permission.

Acknowledgments

I would like to thank my wife Karen and my daughter
Stephanie for their advice, encouragement and proofreading.
I also thank my daughter Catherine for the creation of the
cover design. I express special gratitude to Philip Cutajar and
Paul Thigpen for their proofreading, editing, and scores of
helpful suggestions.

Family Life Center Publications
22226 Westchester Blvd.
Port Charlotte, FL 33952
www.familylifecenter.net

Dedication

Dedicated to Karen

My heartfelt thanks

. . . for saying "yes" when I asked

. . . for being my best friend and covenant partner

. . . for being the mother of our children

"A good wife is the crown of her husband."

PROVERBS 12:4

Contents

A Word of Introduction

Who wants to be bound to a lifetime of unhappiness? Today, men are increasingly pessimistic about finding satisfying, life-long love in marriage. The high rate of divorce has eroded expectations for the possibility of permanent commitment. Increasingly, men are either postponing marriage or are hesitant about ever committing to it. Some cultural observers say that we are on the verge of a post-marriage culture, where marriage is viewed as unnecessary and even unwelcome.

Yet contemporary research shows that marriage is extremely good for men.[1] Married men live longer, and are healthier, happier, and better off financially. No wonder the Bible says, "A good wife . . . is far more precious than jewels" (Proverbs 31:10).

Except for the decision to make Jesus Christ the Lord of your life, choosing a wife is the most important decision you will ever make. My hope is that you carefully use this book to take wise steps towards building a successful, deeply fulfilling, and happy marriage.

It's fully possible in today's world to find and marry a woman who will be your best friend and your covenant partner, who will faithfully love you "till death do you part." Amidst the wasteland of shattered marriages, you *can* find happiness in lasting marital love.

Things work best when you use them as originally intended. I keep warning my younger children that cabinet hinges will bend if used as swings, arms of chairs will crack if used as stools, and beds will break if used as trampolines.

Similarly, over the course of the twentieth century we've ignored God's original intent, His design, for lasting love. This neglect has created a desert of broken marriages, as well as a mountain of incredible heartache. Happiness in marriage begins long before you say, "I do." By rediscovering and practicing the divine design for courtship *before* marriage, you'll help ensure lasting love and fulfillment *in* marriage.

The sources I used to write this book were many: Scripture, Church teachings about marriage, timeless wisdom from past generations, contemporary research on marriage and family life, my personal experiences from twenty-five years of marriage, and my experience helping other married people in counseling— along with a healthy dose of common sense.

I found the idea for the *ABCs of Choosing a Good Wife* in a three-thousand-year-old portion of the Old Testament. In Proverbs chapter 31, a queen mother teaches her son the characteristics to look for in a wife. Verses 10 through 31 present an acrostic poem in Hebrew; that is, each verse begins with a letter of the Hebrew alphabet in alphabetical order. This literary device was used to project an "A-to-Z" picture of the ideal wife for the guidance of the royal prince.

You'll find the ABCs direct and challenging, but they can serve as a template for your selection of a wife. I'm confident that by following *all* the ABCs, you can lessen the likelihood of divorce by at least seventy-five percent. Remember this, however: There's more to making a successful marriage than choosing a good wife. It takes two to make a strong marriage. So I've also included material to help you be a good husband and father. Your marriage will not benefit if all you do is read this book; you have to put into practice what you learn.

CHAPTER ONE

A

Attraction

John Blanchard stood up from his seat and straightened his neatly pressed army uniform as he studied the crowd of people making their way through Grand Central Station in New York. He eagerly looked for the girl whose heart he knew, but whose face he didn't—the girl with the rose.

His interest in her had begun two years before in a Florida library. Taking a book off the shelf, he found himself intrigued, not with the words of the book, but with the notes penciled in the margins.

The soft handwriting reflected a thoughtful soul and an insightful mind. In the front of the book, he discovered the previous owner's name: Miss Holly Maynell. In time and with some effort he located her address. She now lived in New York City.

He wrote her a letter introducing himself and inviting her to correspond. The next week he was shipped overseas for duty in World War II.

During the next two years they grew to know each other through overseas mail. Each letter was a seed falling on a fertile heart. A romance was budding. Blanchard requested a photograph, but she refused. She felt that, if he really cared, it wouldn't matter what she looked like.

When the day finally came for him to return from Europe, they scheduled their first meeting at 7:00 P.M. at the train station. "You'll recognize me," she wrote, "by the red rose I'll be wearing on my lapel." So at 7:00 P.M. sharp he was in the station looking for the girl whose heart he loved, but whose face he'd never seen.

In Mr. Blanchard's words, this is what happened next:

> A gorgeous young woman was coming toward me, her figure long and slim. Her blond hair lay back in curls from her delicate ears; her eyes were as blue as flowers. Her lips and chin had a gentle firmness, and in her pale green suit she was like springtime come alive.
>
> I started toward her, entirely forgetting to notice that she was not wearing a rose. As I moved, a small smile curved her lips. "Going my way, soldier?" she murmured. Almost uncontrollably I made one step closer to her—and then I saw Holly Maynell.
>
> She was standing almost directly behind the girl. A woman well past forty, she had graying hair tucked under a worn hat. She was more than plump, with her thick-ankled feet thrust into low-heeled shoes. The girl in the green suit was walking quickly away. I felt as though I was split in two, so keen was my

desire to follow her, and yet so deep was my longing for the woman whose spirit had truly been my companion overseas.

And there she stood. Her pale, plump face was gentle and sensible; her gray eyes had a warm and kindly twinkle. I did not hesitate. My fingers gripped the small, worn copy of the book that was to identify me to her.

This would not be love, but it would be something precious, something perhaps better than love, a friendship for which I had been and must ever be grateful. I squared my shoulders, saluted, and held out the book to the woman, even though while I spoke I felt choked by the bitterness of my disappointment. "I'm Lieutenant John Blanchard, and you must be Miss Maynell. I am so glad we could meet; may I take you to dinner?"

The woman's face broadened into a tolerant smile. "I don't know what this is about, Son," she answered, "but the young lady in the green suit who just went by, she begged me to wear this rose on my coat. And she said that if you were to ask me out to dinner, I should tell you that she is waiting for you in the big restaurant across the street. She said it was some kind of test!"[2]

Fatal attractions

Miss Maynell was a wise woman. She realized that many men are blindly attracted to a pretty face without regard to what's inside. It's a fatal mistake to be attracted to a woman just for her looks, without knowing and loving her as a person.

A scenario in contrast to that of Miss Maynell and Lieutenant Blanchard might go something like this: At the first sight of Laurie walking across campus in her form-fitting sweater and hip-hugging jeans, Barry's breath is taken away. He instantly falls in love and decides that he wants her for his wife, imagining perpetual bliss in a marriage to such a beautiful woman.

Laurie is flattered that Barry is so strongly attracted to her. They are engaged during college, and both decide to work for a year before getting married. Barry starts his insurance career, and Laurie works as the weather girl at a local TV station.

Just a couple of years after an extravagant wedding, their stormy marriage has made them both miserable. Barry can't figure out why the woman who had so powerfully attracted him now upsets and repulses him. After enduring four years of misery, Barry files for divorce and tries to obtain custody of his twin daughters. Despite spending $65,000 in a bitter dispute, his attorneys fail to win custody for him. Barry is left alone, bitter, and broke.

On the surface, a pretty woman can seem incredibly appealing. Yet choosing a wife without the inner qualities to match her attractiveness is a potential plunge into a pit of misery. The Bible warns a young man in choosing a wife that "charm is deceitful, and beauty is vain" (Proverbs 31:30). A gorgeous woman is no guarantee of marital happiness.

The importance attached to physical attractiveness in choosing a mate soared during the last half of the twentieth century, fueled by the explosive growth of the visual media and the cosmetics industry.[3] This shift in social attitudes created such superficial mate selection criteria that we now value looks more than character, virtues, and actions. Warning against such superficiality, the Bible says, "Like a gold ring in a swine's snout is a beautiful woman without discretion" (Proverbs 11:22).

Make an ugly woman your wife?

Jimmy Soul's number-one hit song in 1963 declared, "If you want to be happy for the rest of your life, make an ugly woman your wife." Jimmy Soul didn't really believe that you had to marry an ugly woman in order to be happily married. Yet his classic rock song made an obvious over-statement to underscore an important truth: Marriage to a beautiful woman lacking inner beauty is a ticket to marital misery.

The important question: How can you find a beautiful wife–both inside and out?

Make a modest woman your wife

My rendition of Jimmy Soul's song is this: "If you want to be happy for the rest of your life, make a modest woman your wife." Modesty is the mysterious veil over a woman's outward beauty that allows you to see her inner beauty as well.

It's incredibly easy for a woman wearing skin-tight, revealing clothing to dazzle you. Be aware that many immodest women are literally "letting it all hang out"; that is, they have nothing in the way of inner beauty to offer you. Immodesty can be a way of compensating for a lack of inner character and virtue. Lack of modesty can also be a tip-off that a woman has low self-esteem.

God designed a woman's body to radiate more beauty than any of His other works. He intends for a wife's body to be physically appealing. Yet God also designed a woman's body as a sacred mystery to be unveiled only to her husband—not to every other guy gawking as she passes by. To *profane* means to make common what God has set apart as sacred. A lack of modesty in a very real way profanes the sacredness of a woman's body.

To prevent the fatal attraction to a pretty woman capable of only superficial love, you should never consider choosing— even for a moment—an immodest woman for a wife. Modesty in an attractive woman allows you to discern the inner beauty that makes for a satisfying marriage. Your happiness in marriage depends on your choosing a woman with the treasure of inward beauty.

CHAPTER TWO

B

Before You Say, "I Do"... Beware of the "Trigger Effect"

You were thrilled to meet, fall in love with, and marry Mrs. Right. You didn't spend much time learning about her parents and family experiences. Why bother? You found her to be an attractive, funny, caring, and kind soul mate during your dating.

So you were shocked a few months after the honeymoon, or after the birth of your first child, when she seemed to change dramatically—for the worse. Now she doesn't even seem to be the woman you married. What happened?

I call it the "trigger effect." Many people have unresolved childhood conflicts lying dormant inside them. Even couples who live together before marriage, mistakenly thinking that such an arrangement is the best way to get to know each other deeply, often find that these conflicts remain hidden. But the pivotal events of marriage or the birth of a child have the potential to trigger their reappearance unexpectedly. The result can be monumental personal and marital difficulties, such as eating disorders, inability to demonstrate affection, uncontrollable anger, irritability, serious depression, or alcoholism.

The surprising impact of past family life

Obviously, you want to minimize the possibility that the trigger effect could explode in your marriage. To save yourself a life of misery, then, you must pay attention to this critical truth about family life: *We all bring our past family life into our marriages.* The family backgrounds of both spouses have a continuing impact on their married life, for better or for worse. So you need to investigate carefully the family background of any potential spouse if you don't want to encounter unpleasant surprises when it's too late.

If you or your potential wife come from a family with a history of alcoholism or drug addiction; sexual, physical, or verbal abuse; serious psychological problems; or divorce— then you must be aware that your marriage *will* have additional strains.

You might ask, "How could a divorce in my fiancée's family background possibly affect our future relationship, since we're both Christians committed to lifelong marriage?" Everyone, even a committed Christian, is deeply affected by personal family history. A child's bad family experiences can exert a strong negative influence on her marriage as an adult.

Fatherless daughters

For instance, what happens to a girl later in life when her parents divorce during her childhood? For the three decades following the divorce explosion in the 1960s, most people believed that the impact of divorce on children lasts only a few years. Yet a recent landmark study of the long-term consequences of divorce reported that the impact of parental divorce carries well into young adulthood.[4]

Especially for girls, the impact of divorce can have a "sleeper effect." During her childhood and early teens she may appear to have overcome the impact of her parents' breakup. Then in late adolescence, during courtship, or in the early years of marriage, it all returns with a vengeful force. Many women from divorced families struggle even with the thought of marriage, fearing they are doomed to fall into their parents' template of a failed marriage. For many such women, the slightest problems in marriage can trigger excessive fears that they are destined to repeat their parents' experience.

Through a close identification with her father, a girl matures into womanhood by learning to relate to men in a warm and healthy fashion. But it's often difficult for a girl to feel secure and comfortable in a deep relationship with her husband when she carries a lingering sense that the first man in her life abandoned her. Women who were abandoned by the first man in their life are likely to tell researchers that they are unhappy in their sexual relationship.

If a woman was sexually abused in childhood, not an uncommon problem today, the types of stresses outlined above are even more prone to surface in marriage.

The value of a *good* counselor

What should you do if a woman you're interested in comes from a divorced, dysfunctional, or abusive family background? In the past, I would have just pointed out the potential for additional marital problems. Today, I would issue a strong caution *and* recommend skilled, professional counseling—*before* making a proposal of marriage.

A word of warning about counselors is in order. There are probably more ineffective, incompetent, or dysfunctional marital therapists and psychologists than there are good ones. You're better off without any counseling at all than with bad counseling. Yet the value of a good counselor is priceless to those who require assistance.[5]

Build upon the strengths of other couples

If you, or a woman you are interested in, come from a home shattered by divorce, you need to know that you are not doomed to repeat past family patterns. Millions have overcome negative influences from family background.

You should read the real-life stories of couples from troubled family backgrounds who overcame their past and successfully established their own marriage.[6] Rather than denying any lingering effects from family background, successful couples faced their past, worked through negative family influences, and found a happy married life.

Mentors help couples navigate marital turbulences

Recent research has demonstrated that mentoring couples who informally meet to encourage couples experiencing marital stress are four times more effective than professional marriage counselors in helping such couples stay married. Mentoring couples have experienced the ups and downs of married life and are willing to share their experiences with a younger couple. If you, or a woman you plan to marry, come from a dysfunctional family background, then find and meet regularly with a mentoring couple—during your engagement and throughout the first few years of your marriage. Choose a mentoring couple who has successfully navigated through the marital turbulences associated with family background.

Many people—through heroic efforts, good counsel, and dependence upon God's grace—have learned the skills to cope with their background conflicts. Others think they have magically escaped being scarred by family dysfunction, only to find the sudden and unexpected reappearance of negative behaviors in the first few years of marriage. *Before* you get engaged, find out if anything in the family background has the potential to launch the "trigger effect." If so, then obtain the finest counseling and mentoring available *before* taking any further steps toward marriage.

CHAPTER THREE

C

Cohabitation: Extinguishing *Real* Love—Before Your Marriage Begins

Currently, the average marriage in the U.S. that ends in divorce lasts about seven years. Approximately twenty percent of divorcing couples end their marriage before their third anniversary. In the face of such gloomy statistics, no wonder young people are becoming increasingly pessimistic about marriage. But is the problem really with marriage, or with what goes on before marriage?

"Trial marriages" lead to broken relationships

Anyone can understand why a young couple in our divorce-prone society would want to take precautionary steps to make sure they're really suited for each other. A common way couples do this is by living together in a "trial marriage," to see if they're really compatible. Research shows that the majority of high schoolers and college students think that living together improves their chances for a successful marriage. In fact, more than half the couples getting married today have lived together first, up from ten percent in 1965.

On the surface this seems to make sense. Everyone knows that you take a car out for a test drive before purchasing it. In a similar way, it seems natural to imagine that a "trial" marriage will improve your chances for marital success.

In reality, however, the opposite is likely to occur. Striking statistical evidence shows that if you have sex before marriage, you'll *increase* the odds of divorce by at least forty-five percent![7]

Research by The Marriage Project at Rutgers University found that cohabiting couples are more prone to develop negative individualistic attitudes that undermine genuine love. The Marriage Project also found that cohabiting couples are less happy in marriage and less sexually fulfilled and faithful to their partners than couples who did not live together before marriage. Only one in six cohabiting couples enjoys a relationship that lasts longer than three years.[8]

Unexpected problems from cohabitation

Cohabitation destroys love and marriage for at least four reasons.[9]

First, living together kills trust and commitment. Since cohabiting relationships are usually brief, these men and women inevitably go through repeated heart-wrenching breakups. Author Barbara Dafoe Whitehead states that "each successive relationship starts out at a lower level of trust and commitment than the one before."[10] These downwardly spiraling cycles cannot help but weaken trust and commitment, two of the ingredients necessary for a successful marriage.

Second, cohabitation creates selfishness—the enemy of true love. The marital embrace is designed by God to be a total, self-giving experience. So before you enter the marital embrace, you need to take the vital step of pledging yourself in the marriage vows.

Exchanging vows is not just a nice touch at a wedding ceremony. These vows mysteriously and profoundly cement your souls together in the deepest part of your being. The self-giving and mutual joining, expressed through your vows, need to precede the self-giving of the marital embrace. When the pleasure of sexual relations is sought apart from the vows of lifelong love and fidelity, then this embrace is degraded into an act of selfishness. Escalating frictions and bitterness often accompany such selfishness.

Third, cohabitation increases the probability of divorce because of its effect on marital communication. A primary way you'll give love to your wife is through verbal communication. Women have a deep and continuing need to receive verbal expressions of love from their husbands.

You're headed for marital disaster if you are like the guy who said to his wife, "Look, I told you when we got married that I love you, and if I ever change my mind, I'll let you know." Premarital relations increase the chances that you will be permanently tongue-tied. A study by the National Council on Family Relations found that newlywed wives who had engaged in premarital relations complained of poor communication after the wedding.[11]

The need for premarital communication

Why is this true? For starters, you must realize that there's a vast difference between the communication styles of men and women. Simply put, men talk far less than women about feelings. I'm sure that this isn't much of a surprise.

During the critically important months before marriage, you need to learn how to overcome your natural reluctance to express love to your fiancée in verbal ways. Sure, you'll feel physical urges. But if these are restrained through mutual self-control, your verbal skills will have a chance to develop.

On the other hand, if you engage in physical relations before marriage, the overwhelming intensity of physical communication will eclipse the verbal. You won't be able to imagine what "better" communication could possibly take place. Thus, at the very stage in your developing relationship when emotional bonding through verbal communication should be flourishing, you will end up with fast-frozen communication skills.

After about seven years of waiting for the big thaw (that never takes place), millions of wives lose all hope of ever receiving emotional support from their husbands. Many of them file for divorce. The divorcing wife says, "You don't love me," while the baffled husband is without a clue as to what happened.

Fourth, cohabitation entraps couples in its bonding dynamics. There is no such thing as a one-night fling, or a casual live-in relationship. God designed all sexual relations to cause a strong union between persons. Pre-marital sexual relations cause escalating attachments—often to the wrong person.

Why did he do it?

When I served in the Navy I was puzzled to see normal, handsome sailors deciding to marry so-called "bar hogs": the ugly, crude, morally loose, and overweight prostitutes they met in bars. (Please pardon the crude Navy term.) A conniving "bar hog" married to one of my shipmates hired a hit-man to have her husband killed so she could collect his modest serviceman's insurance policy. Fortunately, the murder plot was exposed to the police by the hit man, but I couldn't help wondering: Why in the world would a man want to marry a woman like this?

This foolish sailor was entrapped and deluded by the bonding dynamic that takes place in pre-marital sexual relations. St. Paul described this dynamic in his warning to Christians living in ancient Corinth, a seaport known around the world for its sexual immorality:

> Do you not know that your bodies are members of Christ? Shall I therefore take the members of Christ and make them members of a prostitute? Never! Do you not know that he who joins himself to a prostitute becomes one body with her? For, as it is written, "The two shall become one flesh" (1 Corinthians 6:15–16).

While my former shipmate's behavior may be an extreme example of how the sexual bonding dynamic can cloud judgment, the process is repeated to a lesser degree by millions of men every year, who find themselves married to women they would never have chosen otherwise.

Cancerous relationships

Cohabitation's bonding dynamic operates like cancer cells growing out of control. It causes commitments to grow and bonding to take place which never should have begun. Blame no one but yourself if you make a disastrous choice in a life partner because of lustful passions.

Extinguishing *real* love–before your marriage begins

Why extinguish real love in your marriage before it begins? Avoid cohabitation. It's one of the stupidest things you can do to mess up your marriage. If you're currently in a cohabiting relationship, then put down this book and make a change immediately. I mean right now! Take whatever steps are necessary to end cohabitation. Recovering a chaste courtship will dramatically improve your chances for a successful marriage.

God's commandments are for *your* good

Before God gave His commandments, He wasn't up in heaven wondering, "How can I mess up people's lives and rob them of happiness and pleasure?" No, the Bible says that God gave us His commandments for our good (Deuteronomy 10:13). God's commandment to reserve sexual intimacy for marriage is His gracious safeguard for true love. Keep to His path and find lasting happiness in marriage.

CHAPTER FOUR

D

Dating or Courtship?

Dating creates a series of temporary, emotionally-based, romantic relationships. "Going steady" intensifies dating relationships by creating "mini-engagements," as well as the subsequent heartbreaks caused by "mini-divorces." Is dating's pattern of bonding and breaking up a better preparation for lifelong marriage, or for today's familiar cycle of marriage, divorce, and remarriage?

Dating only as old as the automobile

Dating is mainly a twentieth-century phenomenon. You might be surprised to learn that the history of dating is no older than the automobile.

One book on the demise of courtship is aptly titled *From Front Porch to Back Seat*.[12] The automobile took young couples and courtship away from their families. While providing what seemed to be exciting new freedoms, it had disastrous consequences for marriage.

Dating leaves out the family

Dating usually involves very little time with families and much more time alone as a couple or with peers. Only in "enlightened" societies have people been crazy enough to think this is a good preparation for enduring marriage. For the rest of the history of the world, and in all cultures, the family circle was recognized as the best environment to get to know a potential marriage partner.

Double-dating (frequently double trouble)

Time away alone together, or even with peers, is prime time for premarital sex. The more time alone together, the higher the probability of premarital relations. Some chastity "experts" imagine that double-dating is the perfect deterrent to immorality in dating. But the reality is that double-dating with peers is usually "double trouble."

Courtship within the family circle

The separation from family during dating removes all the protective guidance a mother and father can offer. In contrast, all the strength of the family is placed at your disposal during courtship. Unlike dating, courtship takes place in the context of family life. It's a relationship between a young man and a young woman who are seeking a partner for marriage.

Exactly how do you court in the twenty-first century? The skills needed for the art of courtship have been lost, and we all need to rediscover them. For starters, you can rethink how you use a car.

I know this sounds radical, but I suggest that a car be used only for chaperoned social activities and to visit each other's

homes, if they are nearby. You, and the woman you are courting, should interact with your families at mealtimes and join
in family activities, recreation, and outings as much as possible. Don't use a car for private times together. Your family
should provide some semi-private "space," such as the family room or the front porch, for the two of you to talk together.

Courtship and communication

Verbal communication is a primary way that husbands *should*
express love for their wives. Yet the lack of genuine communication by men in marriage is deeply troubling to millions of wives. As we saw in chapter three, it is a prime reason why women decide to give up on their marriages and
divorce their husbands.

You'll never learn how to express your feelings if your communication consists mainly in steaming up the back of a car.
Get your relationship out of the back seat and return it to the
front porch, where real love can be communicated.

College courtship

What if your family's home is far away? It's hardly unusual
today for young persons to live some distance from their
family. But few have considered the impact of the loss of
immediate family support for young people trying to find a
marriage partner. If college or some other necessity takes
you away from your family, you'd be wise to seek out a
"mentoring couple" who can become actively involved in
your courtship process away from home.

Organizations such as Marriage Savers are having fantastic
success using mentoring couples in churches. These mentors assist couples during engagement and in the early years

of marriage.[13] In chapter 2, we recommended a mentoring couple strategy as a must for those with divorce and dysfunctional family backgrounds. Why not extend this extremely successful strategy to all courting couples as well? Your mentoring couple might be a faculty couple or a couple you meet in a local parish.

Should you find courtship mentors, keep in mind that they should never totally supplant your own parents in this role. I suggest that you use your vacations to court within your immediate family circle. You'd also be wise to consult your parents when choosing a mentoring couple; you'll want the best example of a loving, Christian family for this important role.

If your family isn't nearby, or a committed mentoring couple isn't available, then at least you can spend your courting time together in chaperoned group social activities. For instance, if you're away at college, a few courting couples could go out to dinner with a young faculty couple for an enjoyable evening.

Preserving physical intimacy for marriage

I can just hear it now. "Chaperones! You've got to be kidding. Aren't chaperones for little kids' dances and for people who lived in the Dark Ages?"

No, chaperones have been appreciated by wise people in every age—people who realize that it's all too easy for even a Christian couple to become physically intimate before marriage, thereby weakening their relationship. Using a chaperone is one of the time-tested methods of preserving physical intimacy for marriage. It's valued by those who treasure lasting love.

Chaperones and the family courting circle were abandoned in the early twentieth century for the thrill of the automobile and the "independence" provided by the dating revolution. Is it any wonder that throughout the last century the incidences of premarital sexuality skyrocketed, leaving millions of broken hearts, shattered families, and fatherless children? Isn't it past time that we return to the practices that directly involve families and chaperones in preserving lasting love?

Dads elevate the courting relationship

Even if you're away at college, you should ask the young woman's father for his permission before you start any serious courting. It may sound overly strict or passé, but this time-honored practice will transform your relationship. Calling her father for permission—even though you might be a little nervous—will elevate your courting relationship to a different and higher plane. As you bring the woman's father into your courting relationship, you will increasingly see her as a man's daughter who is worthy of being treated with respect and not as a plaything on a disposable date.

It's also important that you honor her father's advice and authority. Remember, you will be a father one day. Respect her father the way you would want to be respected, and treat the woman you are courting the way you would want *your* daughter treated.

The dating game vs. seeking God's will

Dating is typically done just for the fun of it, without marriage in mind. It's only a game between the sexes. But courtship is much more.

The purpose of courtship is to discover whether it's really God's will for a couple to enter marriage.

Courtship will gain popular appeal in our culture as positive results are demonstrated in the lives of twenty-first century "courtship pioneers." We should start seeing the verifiable beneficial results of courtship, such as fewer divorces and higher marital satisfaction, within a decade or two. In the meantime, if you want your future marriage to last a lifetime, and you don't want to become another "dating game" statistic, then be among those who have chosen the courtship path—the path leading to lifelong marriages.

Courtship and men of gallantry

I deeply believe that men are capable of great gallantry. But Christians often underestimate men's potential.

The organization called Promise Keepers absolutely amazed thousands of pastors (and wives) who never dreamed that so many men would respond to a challenge to be men of integrity. When I began St. Joseph's Covenant Keepers, many people I spoke with couldn't imagine that young Catholic men would respond to a firm challenge to raise the standard in their marriages and family life.

What has been the result? I've personally seen thousands of men respond to the high calling of following Jesus. Men have written us from over fifty foreign countries wanting to know more about the challenge of St. Joseph's Covenant Keepers. Will younger single men respond to a similar challenge? Absolutely. They just need a big enough challenge.

Asking for too little of a commitment doesn't tap into God-given manhood. Yet courtship provides a ringing challenge that can awaken the best and deepest parts of your manhood.

Rather than being a semi-barbarian fixated on self and taking advantage of women, you can become a gallant man, self-sacrificing for the welfare of the woman in your life.

Courtship and modern knighthood

The word pictures suggested by courtship go back to the royal court where a young knight or prince would woo a maiden. Courtship is associated with the chivalry and honor of knighthood. Words such as courage, character, honor, gallantry, sacrifice, magnanimity, virtue, integrity, fidelity, and courtesy (the last word means literally "a court-like politeness"), are not just nice expressions. They're calls to action that can inspire you to greatness. A knight knew who he was and what he stood for.

What will women think of courtship?

Every girl dreams of that special knight who will appear and claim her as his own forever. The behavior of most men in recent generations has caused such dreams to dissipate. When gallant men of character and virtue show up again, women will be excited to be courted by one.

Will you be someone's knight in shining armor? Are you ready to respond to the call of courtship?

Choose your path to marriage

There are two paths for modern mate selection. Along one path lie the flimsy and seldom-lasting dating relationships in which young men treat women merely as objects for personal pleasure and fulfillment. On the higher courtship path, you'll become a real man—a man of gallantry seeking a soul mate to love and cherish in the lifelong sacrament of marriage.

CHAPTER FIVE

E

Earlier or Later Marriage?

Americans are generally waiting longer to get married than in previous generations. For men, the median age of first marriage in 2000 was 26.8, up from 22.8 in 1950. For women, the median age in 2000 was 25.1, up from 20.3 in 1950.

The four main reasons for the delay of marriage in America are what I call the "four C's": (1) Collapse of confidence in marriage, (2) Cohabitation, (3) Career, and (4) Cash (that is, efforts to accumulate money before marriage).

Collapse of confidence

The staggering divorce rate has caused a profound pessimism in the younger generation about the possibility of a lifelong marriage. This collapse of confidence is causing many to hesitate entering what is perceived to be a risky commitment. As we have noted, many erroneously believe that cohabitation will set their insecurities at rest by providing a "trial marriage." This partially explains why "the odds of cohabiting are more than double for those whose parents divorced, compared to those whose parents remained married."[14]

Cohabitation killing incentive

Cohabitation rates have skyrocketed over the past few decades. Cohabitation kills the incentive for marriage, especially for men. Why get married when you can enjoy the benefits without the responsibilities?

Career development for a complex workforce

Lengthy education and other training is often a requirement for a successful career in an increasingly complex working world. It used to be that marriage typically followed college. For many today, there is a whole new stage of life between college and marriage that is totally focused on climbing the career ladder.

Cash is king

Our materialistic culture says, "Don't wait to have it all." Young people are not immune from our "cash is king" culture. As a result, many are seeking to build up assets, fill retirement accounts, and purchase real estate before marriage.

These four C's are pushing up the age of first marriage to historic levels. But Christian couples should listen to the advocates of earlier marriage before following these cultural trends.

An early Church advocate of earlier marriage

One of the strongest advocates for earlier marriage was St. John Chrysostom, the fifth-century Patriarch of Constantinople—perhaps the greatest preacher who ever lived. In his homily on 1 Thessalonians 4:3–7, he forcefully warns his listeners against the dangers of delayed marriage:

> But at the season of marriage, let no one defer it. Behold, I speak the words of a matchmaker, that you should let your sons marry. . . . When your son is grown up, before he enters upon warfare, or any other course of life, consider his marriage. And if he sees that you will soon take a bride for him, and that the time intervening will be short, he will be able to endure the flame [of passion] patiently. But if he perceives that you are remiss and slow, and wait until he acquires a large income, and then you will contract a marriage for him, despairing at the length of the time, he will readily fall into fornication. But alas! the root of evil here also is the love of money. Therefore I exhort you first to regulate well their souls. If he finds his bride chaste, and knows her body alone, then his desire will be vehement, and his fear of God the greater, and the marriage truly honorable, receiving bodies pure and undefiled.[15]

A modern case for earlier marriage

A modern voice recommending earlier marriage is that of The Rev. Michael Orsi.[16] Based upon his pastoral experience, here is a list of some deficiencies he associates with later marriages:

- Later marriage is a major cause of the breakdown in sexual ethics.

- It allows self-centeredness to solidify in the personality, prolongs adolescence, and delays maturity.

- Promiscuity during the 20s and later leads to a weakened married life.

- Later marriage wreaks havoc on souls stemming from promiscuity and impurities.

- Delayed marriages often increase fears of commitment.

- Waiting to get married until life is a third over is unhealthy and unnatural.

- The number of marital prospects diminishes appreciably after one's 25th birthday.

- Prolonged warehousing of adult children at home or in college doesn't do them much good.

Rev. Orsi recommends an ideal marriage age for most between 18 and 25, encouraging men to marry closer to the higher age. But before we form any conclusions about this matter, we need to hear as well from those who recommend *delaying* the age of marriage.

Deciding too young

The divorce rate for those getting married between 21 and 22 years old is exactly double the divorce rate of those marrying at 24 or 25.[17] Teenage marriages have the highest probability of divorce. The widely acknowledged fact that early marriage is associated with high levels of divorce is the most compelling reason for building a case for delaying marriage.

Yet not all early marriages end in divorce. In many cultures with low divorce rates, teenage weddings are common. Most biblical scholars think that in the model for all Christian families, the Holy Family, Mary was a teenager when she was married to Joseph.

So what is it about early marriages in our culture that contributes to such high rates of divorce?

There are three main culprits.

Too little family income

First, too little or too much income matters in marriage. A Stanford University study on the economic influences on divorce found high divorce rates among couples at lower income levels who married early.[18] Couples requiring government financial support had twice the divorce rates of couples who didn't require such assistance. Increases in income, especially that of the husband, lower the probability of divorce —until a high income level is reached. Surprisingly, high incomes were found to be as destabilizing to marriage as low income levels.[19]

We learn from this study that it is important to get your earning potential established before marriage, but also that "getting rich before getting married" is equally destabilizing. An earlier marriage and economic stability is possible if a young man begins preparing to support a family before it is commonly done today.

In biblical times, a Jewish boy crossed over into manhood at age 12. It was the age he became "a son of the Law" and when he chose a trade. The teen years were spent preparing for the responsibilities of family life.

Rather than echoing the accelerated maturity of biblical days, today's teen years are a time of suspended maturity. The result is that young men often don't give serious thought to the necessary preparations to support a family until they are ready to propose. Others don't get in gear for supporting a family until after they are married, and some wait until the first child shows up.

With the assistance of their fathers and educational institutions, it would be wiser for young men to begin earlier training to support a family. Why should marriage be increasingly delayed to accomodate a *Peter Pan* culture?

Delayed development of self-identity

It is important to know who you are and what you want to do in life before you can make a wise choice of a life partner. Many young people don't develop a sense of who they are as an individual, or know their life calling until their mid-twenties. It is a wise idea to delay marriage until this self-identifying task is completed. Yet here too we need to get over the suspended animation of the teen years. Self-identity can mature during the teen years by utilizing wise spiritual direction, career counseling, and a balanced combination of good personality, aptitude, and career testing instruments.[20]

Teen lovers know better than parents

Mark Twain is alleged to have said, "When I was a boy of 14, my father was so ignorant I could hardly stand to have the old man around. But when I got to be 21, I was astounded at how much he had learned in seven years."

One of the reasons for marital success for older couples may be the perceived increase in the parents' wisdom that comes with age. Love songs assert that teen lovers know better than parents. Yet how many teen marriages, fueled by one or both spouses fleeing a troubled family background, run into the "trigger effect" (see chapter 2)? Chapter 8 will show the importance of obtaining parental approval from both spouses' parents for a satisfying marriage. I imagine that a lower divorce rate would accompany teen marriages that begin with courting in the family circle, and proceed towards marriage with the advice and blessings of parents.

Ideal age for marriage?

For those with sufficient financial security, emotional maturity, and parental approval, I encourage consideration of *earlier* marriages (roughly ages 20 to 25). In most situations, it is probably a wise recommendation for men to marry closer to 25 than 20. On the other hand, I discourage what I would call *early* marriage—that is, before the age of 20. Teen marriages seem too great a risk, at least in our culture.

Remember, this suggested ideal age for marriage is only a general guideline. Each individual and each couple has myriad unique factors to weigh. For example, certain professions require lengthy training that might require modifications.

The purpose of courtship is to discover whether it's really God's will for a couple to enter marriage. For that reason, courtship presupposes that both the man and the woman are spiritually, emotionally, and financially ready for marriage. Whatever your age, you are ready to begin courting when you have the maturity to enter marriage and are skilled enough to begin supporting a family.

CHAPTER SIX

F

Family Finances

There's no escaping the reality: Money matters in marriage. The number-one topic in marital fights is money. Husbands and wives commonly develop bitterness toward each other over family finances. Due to a relatively new economic situation in history, there is now one big decision you need to make before marriage, so that a particular money squabble over this issue doesn't escalate into a domestic war that ends in divorce.

The big decision

During the last half of the twentieth century, America completed the transformation to an economy of dual-wage earner families. Today, the prices of expensive items such as homes, private schools, and college educations, as well as everyday items such as dining out, health care, insurance, and amusement park visits, are based on the assumption that the average family will have two wages to afford them.

Your big decision is to decide *before* courtship and marriage whether you plan to follow this contemporary model of family life—or adopt the historic model of a single breadwinner. Whatever your decision, it needs to be made in light of the new economic realities.

Your decision will have huge implications for the structure of your family. I can't tell you which choice to make, but I can give you a series of questions related to motherhood and nurturing children that can assist you in making an informed decision:

- How important is it for a mother to be home with preschool children?

- Do you have health concerns associated with daycare and preschools?[21]

- Do you have concerns about negative socialization in daycare?[22]

- How important is it for a mother to be home in the afternoons for school-aged children and teens?[23]

- How important is it for a mother to have all her energies available for nurturing children?

- Do you have a desire to be a homeschooling family?

Mothers find it extremely difficult to pursue a demanding full-time career outside the home and to nurture children to their potential at the same time. So carefully determine your priorities. Motherhood, especially in a large family, is a full-time, demanding, and yet deeply fulfilling vocation. If you want your wife to be free to join the rapidly-growing ranks of mothers leaving the full-time workplace to stay home, then you'll have be a good provider.

Count the cost

Jesus said, "Which of you, desiring to build a tower, does not first sit down and count the cost?" (Luke 14:28). The single vs. dual-career choice could literally be a million-dollar decision for some families (when you multiply an annual salary times the number of nurturing years). You'll have to weigh the costs and the benefits carefully.

A substantial number of women would be frustrated not to be in the workforce, even if they were mothers with younger children. They not only desire the thousands of dollars in income over two or three decades, but the career satisfaction as well. It would be unfair for you to expect a woman desiring a lifelong career to be a stay-at-home mom. In fairness, you should get emotionally involved only with a woman who shares your choice in the "big decision."

One of the most pressing concerns facing modern families is to find ways that allow mothers to devote all their energies to service in the home. It has been wisely said that "the issue today is generally not the right of women to enter the workforce or to follow a career. The pressing question is that of finding ways for working wives and mothers to carry out their irreplaceable service within the family."[24]

If you and the woman you plan to marry are in agreement that she should be a stay-at-home mom, then the responsibility for making this a possibility falls chiefly on your shoulders. How do you plan to make this happen?

Be a dual-wage earner

Our economic structure will probably not return to a family wage during your lifetime. In the midst of America's wealth, fathers are finding it increasingly difficult to make a decent living. Nearly a third of American men aged 25 to 34 do not earn enough to keep a family with two children above the poverty line.[25] Therefore, you will have to do something unusual in order to provide for a family on a single paycheck.

What I offer is a personal suggestion, not a rigid position. This advice is what I would give a good friend or close family member. It is yours to freely accept or reject.

I suggest that you develop the skills to be a dual-wage earner. I am not talking about regularly working double shifts that would tear you away from your family. You need a job that allows for adequate time with your family. I am talking about choosing a career that enables you to earn an upper-middle-class income to provide for a middle-class lifestyle. An alternative is to earn a middle-class income for a lower-middle-class lifestyle. One of these alternatives seems like a logical way of supporting a family today with a single paycheck.

A prudent warning to those who might be content with a lower-middle-class lifestyle: You need to ensure that you set your financial goals high enough so that you are not crushed by the constantly increasing costs of raising a family. Our electric bill today is more than twice the amount of the monthly mortgage payment we made on our first home. My family's annual health and dental insurance costs today are almost as large as my entire annual salary when we were first married.

It's wise not to get a late start in preparations to become a provider in today's "family unfriendly" economy. A young man desiring to be a good provider needs to have all eight cylinders of his earning potential energized and directed towards skills, jobs, careers or professions that will support a family. Early, consistent, and high-quality career counseling can be very helpful. Careful planning will also minimize frequent shifting from job to job and wandering from one career to another, which often lead to problems in providing.

Be aware that career counselors often assume your family will be dual-income. Make your plans known if you desire career planning to help you become the exclusive family breadwinner.

Deciding with your descendants in mind

The six-nation Iroquois confederacy had a law that required every deliberation to consider the impact of the decision on the next seven generations. What a great family decision-making perspective! Elevate the horizon in your family decision-making so you can envision the long-term impact upon your children, grandchildren, and great grandchildren. What will be the inter-generational result of your "big decision"?

What about being rich?

This may sound un-American, but a prayer in Proverbs says: "Give me neither poverty nor riches; feed me with the food that is needful for me, lest I be full, and deny Thee, and say, 'Who is the LORD?' or lest I be poor, and steal, and profane the name of my God" (Proverbs 30:8–9). Family stability is enhanced when your family's finances avoid extremes. It's fine if wealth comes your way, but don't strive to get rich. Striving after money and piling up excessive wealth often pierces the hearts of married couples and creates problems in raising children.

What about being Mr. Mom?

Except for serious health problems, and for temporary arrangements while the husband learns advanced skills to increase his earning potential, it's usually best that the husband not depend upon his wife as the primary breadwinner of the family. Wisdom in the book of Sirach says, "There is wrath and impudence and great disgrace when a wife supports her husband" (25:22). One study found that a $5,000 increase in a wife's earnings after marriage increased the odds of divorce or separation by five percent.[26]

Money affects the heart, and the heart affects marriage

Every couple needs to maintain constant vigilance against an inordinate love of money. If you allow money to displace the love of God in your hearts, then marital love evaporates as well. Honoring God with your money by tithing is an effective aid in balancing your perspective on money.[27]

If you are like most men, you'll find it difficult to keep a balanced perspective on money. In part that's because God calls men to be the main providers in the home. He expects you to work hard, providing for your family as part of your Christian responsibilities. And that means making money must become a big part of your focus.

The flip side of this issue is that many men go overboard as they turn making a living into an all-consuming desire to make a financial killing. A man with the priorities of money and career first, golf and football second, wife, children, and God a distant third, is sure to make a lousy husband. Your life priorities should be God, family, work—in that order.

In contrast to the many men overly committed to their work, a somewhat smaller number of men simply lack the necessary motivation and drive to support their families. This type of husband creates such huge levels of frustration in his wife that she frequently seeks an outlet—and often that outlet is divorce or separation.

Demonstrate that you're a responsible provider

As you begin courting someone, you should be able to demonstrate that you can support a family and are a skilled worker.[28] Until the disordered days of the late twentieth century, a man never dreamed of seeking a woman's hand in marriage unless he was prepared to demonstrate to her parents—that he was an able provider. An often-overlooked responsibility of a provider is obtaining adequate health and life insurance (which should be equal to ten times annual earnings).

The book of Proverbs says, "Prepare your work outside, get everything ready for you in the field; and after that build your house" (24:27). Translating this wisdom from an agricultural society to our own, it means, "Get your career and earning potential established first, *then* get married and start your family."

This "get prepared in career before marriage" principle also applies to completing educational and vocational training. Education completed, or nearly completed, before marriage strengthens your relationship. In fact, according to one study, "every year of schooling *before* marriage decreases the likelihood of divorce by about four percent. Yet every year of schooling by husband or wife *after* marriage increases the likelihood of divorce by about six percent."[29]

Eliminating debt before marriage

While it's prudent to get your education before getting married, it's also wise to get rid of all consumer debt before tying the knot. Starting a family is financially demanding, especially when babies start arriving. A couple should engage in a full and mutual debt disclosure, ideally before publicly announcing an engagement. Each potential spouse needs to list all outstanding debts. Undisclosed debts can be an irritating sore in marriage.

Your consideration to postpone marriage in order to pay off debts needs to be carefully balanced with concerns for moral purity. Long engagements often carry an increased risk of premarital relations, which weaken faith and family life much more than debts. For that reason, pay attention to the admonition of St. Paul when determining the length of an engagement: "If any one thinks that he is not behaving properly toward his betrothed, if his passions are strong . . . let them marry" (1 Corinthians 7:36).

To have to choose between postponing marriage or entering marriage with consumer debt is less than an ideal situation. As early preparation for successful married life, develop the disciplines necessary to escape attachment to material things and the temptation to accumulate debt. No matter what your income potential may be, the jaws of debt will *always* be ready to consume more than earnings. You want to keep your family free from the corrosive effects of a lifestyle of unrestrained debt.

Finally, what about college loans? Young couples wanting to enter marriage debt-free but facing $25,000 in college loans for each spouse (which now can be obtained with high-interest credit cards) must give serious thought to how and when those loans will be paid off.

Should most of your college loans be paid off before marriage? Yes, with the exception of loans for a professional degree that provides sufficient earning potential to pay them off within a maximum of seven years. Too many young couples cannot afford both paying off college loans and raising children. And as we'll see in the next section, putting off children for the sake of debt is a shaky way to begin marriage.

CHAPTER SEVEN

G

Generosity in the Service of Life

You must ask yourself another crucial question about your future marriage. Your answer will have lasting effects. Here's the second big question: What is the primary purpose of your marriage?

Some possible answers could include highly desirable goals: "to love one another for a lifetime"; "to live happily ever after"; "to share romance"; "to care mutually for each other through all the good times as well as the tough times."

All the above answers are good, but they lack the one chief purpose of marriage that Christians of all centuries until our own have understood—a purpose that's been partially eclipsed in recent generations. In a word, the main purpose of marriage is *kids*. Or to say it the way theologians have for centuries: "The chief end of marriage is the procreation and education of children."

The secret to "living happily ever after"

I doubt there's a man reading this book who doesn't want to experience "living happily ever after" with that special woman who will be his wife. But in order to discover the fullness of marital love, you and your future wife must embrace the secret of the Christian life. Jesus taught that we must lose our lives to find them. He said that the secret to life is not to be served, but to serve *others* and to sacrifice for others (see Matthew 10:39; 20:26–28).

Love is elusive. When we seek to receive it more than to give it, love wanes. To experience love in its fullness, we have to go beyond simply seeking to have our need for love met.

Marital love in all its marvelous depth is only discovered when it goes outside itself. When a husband and wife through their love bring forth new life, their love is dynamically transformed and enriched. Life-giving love is so potent that it becomes visible—in a new person with an eternal destiny. Just look into the face of a new father to see the way fatherhood transforms a man.

Nevertheless, an estimated one third of all young couples in our nation today intend to have no more than one child. What a profound mistake to enter marriage with such plans, or even worse, to avoid having children altogether! Millions of couples regard children as they would a disease, so they take pills to make sure they don't "catch" one.

By willfully rejecting kids, you bottle up precious reserves of love that you'll never savor. (I'm not referring here to those many couples who desire children but can't have them, or who are unable to have all the children they desire. These couples can enrich their marital love by adoption or by special charitable acts to meet the needs of others.)

Yikes! Kids are expensive. They consume your cash, mess up your house, break all your nice stuff, demand all your time, and before leaving home, they frequently crash your cars.

Today many young couples reject parenthood with excuses such as these: "We really aren't ready for kids." "We want to advance in our careers, travel to exotic destinations, and have a rich social life together." "We want to be able to afford the better things in life." "Besides, who wants the embarrassment of a screaming brat throwing temper tantrums in the supermarket cereal aisle?" What kind of priorities do such comments reflect?

Finding happiness in surprising places

What do you want out of marriage? What you really want is to align your marriage as closely as possible to the purposes of God. The closer we align ourselves with our Creator's purposes, the more we find true happiness, fulfillment, and love.

Our Creator seems to have chosen some crazy places to provide fulfillment in marriage: worrying whether the family checkbook will balance with all the bills this month, changing messy diapers, sitting up late at night with a sick child, teaching siblings to get along for the thousandth time. In these challenges, struggles, and sacrifices, however, marital love is most profound, reaching a depth that those in pursuit of personal peace and affluence don't even know exists.

The first words God ever spoke to Adam and Eve were these: "Be fruitful and multiply" (Genesis 1:28). I know that many modern voices, even some from within the Church, proclaim that this is an outmoded notion. I suggest that you plug your ears to all these anti-life mantras. Instead, heed the voice of

God, who hasn't changed His mind about the desirability of children. Jesus still loves the little children very much!

The issue of children is a good subject for a long talk with any prospective wife. Remember, you're not only looking for a good wife for yourself; you're also looking for a good mother for your children.

How many kids?

Many couples want someone to tell them how many kids they should have. But the Church doesn't explicitly insist on a particular number. Instead she encourages all Christian couples to cultivate prayerfully an attitude of generosity in the service of life. Even so, many couples still ask, "How many?"

Let me give you a personal answer. My wife, Karen, and I are the parents of eight children. We've met countless people who go into shock when they see how many children we have. Some think we're freaks for actually wanting so many. We constantly hear comments such as "Are you running a daycare business?" "Haven't you figured out how babies are made yet?" "Are you trying to start a basketball team?"

What will you say at 65?

Actually, we're just living out Christian family life the way it was designed. I can look anyone straight in the eye and say that I wouldn't change places with any other man in the world. I'm a satisfied man. How many D.I.N.K. (those intentionally choosing "Double Income and No Kids") couples do you know who can say that? How many D.I.N.K. couples will be able to say that when they reach age 65 and have a bloated 401(K)—but no grandchildren?

I can't give you a specific number in answer to the "how many kids" question. But the Bible says, "Happy is the man [and woman] who has his quiver full of them!" (Psalm 127:5). How happy and satisfied do you want to be as a result of your sacrifices as a parent?

Once you're married and have a child, pray this prayer a year or two after the birth of each child: "God, do You want us to have one more child? If You do, Lord, please put Your desire in both our hearts, so that our desires match Your desire." Continue this prayer throughout your childbearing years. You can rest assured of an answer to this prayer. St. Paul wrote, "God is at work in you, both to will and to work for His good pleasure" (Philippians 2:13).

Let the little children come to Jesus

The *Catechism of the Catholic Church* says: "By its very nature the institution of marriage and married love is ordered to the procreation and education of the offspring and it is in them that it finds its crowning glory."[30] Across the centuries Jesus still says to couples today, "Let the children come to me, and do not hinder them; for to such belongs the kingdom of heaven" (Matthew 19:14). Align your future marriage closely with this purpose, and you'll discover all of the mystery of marital love.

CHAPTER EIGHT

H

Honor Your Father and Mother

The book of Genesis describes marriage as a transition from one family to another when it says, "Therefore a man leaves his father and his mother and cleaves to his wife, and they become one flesh" (2:24).

For a successful marriage, both a "leaving" and a "cleaving" have to take place. Your future family naturally grows out of, and in a sense continues, the families you and your future wife grew up in. Besides this healthy continuity, there needs to be a positive transition in which you leave behind the primacy of your birth family relationships in order to start your new family.

Too many couples make the unfortunate mistake of trying to cleave without leaving. No, I'm not talking about the person who can't cut the apron strings. I'm referring to the rebellious, bitter, or ungrateful young person who says, "I can't wait to get out of here. I can't stand my parents, their rules, and their lifestyle."

Becoming what we focus upon

Ironically, such a young person will unwittingly take all his negative family experiences into the new marriage. Instead of a healthy and loving severance of the birth family ties, there will be an ongoing negative focus that binds the new marriage to the past. No matter what our intentions are, we tend to become like what we focus upon. Only healthy separations from the birth family allow for the unencumbered creation of a new family.

Your "hinge relationship"

Your relationship with your parents is a "hinge relationship" that colors all your other personal relationships. Look at the order of the Ten Commandments. The Fourth Commandment to honor father and mother is the "hinge" between those dealing with the love of God and those dealing with the love of other people. Similarly, your ability to love each other in your marriage is related to how you honor your parents.

St. Paul, repeating the Fourth Commandment, says, "'Honor your father and mother' (this is the first commandment with a promise), 'that it may be well with you and that you may live long on the earth'" (Ephesians 6:2–3). Be hesitant to go forward with a wedding when you don't have your parents' blessing.

Parental reaction and marital satisfaction

An important study of 5,174 engaged couples found a strong correlation between parental reaction to an upcoming marriage and the satisfaction level of the couple. The figure on the next page shows that, when both sets of parents were not in favor of a proposed marriage, about eighty-eight percent of the couples experienced low levels of marital satis-faction.[31] When one set of parents was opposed to the mar-riage, over seventy percent experienced low satisfaction.[32]

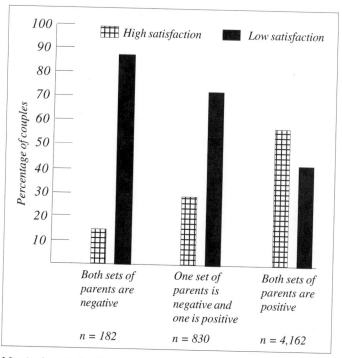

Marital satisfaction compared with parents' reaction to upcoming marriage.

These data indicate that parents have a good internal warn-ing system about potentially unsatisfying relationships. Seek your parents' guidance, listen to their counsel, and obtain their blessing before setting a wedding date. Your parents' advice, coupled with the insights gleaned from the premari-tal inventories described in chapter 12, should be heeded if you really want your married life to be happy and satisfying.

CHAPTER NINE

I

Interfaith vs. Same-Faith Marriages

Daniel is a 32-year-old Marine captain engaged to a pleasant, well-educated, virtuous, and attractive Christian woman. Yet a major problem has erupted with his fiancée. She and her parents attend a church that is openly hostile to his faith.

While Daniel's fiancée has agreed to raise their children within his faith background, she insists that they continue to attend her parents' church on future family visits. But Daniel would never want to expose his children to such antagonistic sermons while visiting his in-laws. This has become a major problem for Daniel and his fiancée, and the wedding is only four months away. How did he get into this predicament?

List courtship commitments *before* developing a relationship

Daniel allowed a relationship to develop before determining his personal courtship commitments (see Appendix I). If you are a person of strong faith, then you will want to guard your heart against starting a relationship with someone who isn't in harmony with your beliefs. Proverbs says, "Keep your heart with all vigilance; for from it flow the springs of life" (4:23).

I suggest that you develop a *written* list of specific standards and commitments as your first step in the process of choosing a wife.[33] It's your "pre-flight" checklist to keep you safely on your marital journey. If you are serious about keeping to your standards, then give your list to an accountability buddy who will hold you to your standards.

Varied outcomes for interfaith marriages

I've heard numerous testimonies from couples in interfaith marriages in which the strong faith of one spouse inspired a conversion experience in the other spouse. Many other interfaith marriages provide opportunities for increased respect, sensitivity, and understanding for each other's beliefs. A number of these couples live happily ever after.

In light of all this, you might ask, "Should I then be unconcerned about faith compatibility in choosing a mate?" To answer that question, you must carefully balance the many stories of successful interfaith marriages against those that didn't end up happily ever after.

The worst loneliness

Marriage at its best is a sharing of the deepest part of your life with your wife. The very worst loneliness is the profound sense of isolation many spouses experience in the midst of their marriages when a partner is unconnected with their faith.

Think about what it might be like sitting in a pew without your wife every Sunday morning for the next forty years. Think about what it might be like never to experience the unifying effect of having you, your wife, and your children praying together.

Do you really want to run such a risk? No wonder St. Paul wisely warns: "Do not be mismated with unbelievers" (2 Corinthians 6:14).

Why risk incompatibility?

A major reason for my writing this book is my strong belief that mountains of marital heartaches (as well as skyrocketing divorce rates) can be dramatically reduced. A shared Christian faith can help you through the turbulent times in marriage. Without a shared belief and value system, you have one more thing to squabble about.

Why run the risk of faith incompatibility? Why choose a marriage in which you're unsure about what her faith will be? The prophet Amos asks: "Do two walk together, unless they have agreed?" (Amos 3:3 NAB). The hazards stemming from mixed marriages should not be underestimated.

A threefold cord

A shared faith is the focal point of marital unity. The book of Ecclesiastes says: "Two are better than one, because they have a good reward for their toil. For if they fall, one will lift up his fellow; but woe to him who is alone when he falls and has not another to lift him up. Again, if two lie together, they are warm; but how can one be warm alone? And though a man might prevail against one who is alone, two will withstand him. A threefold cord is not quickly broken" (4:9–12).

A shared faith is like the third strand of a threefold cord that binds you and your wife, not only in body and mind, but also in soul. For example, it helps with all those difficult adjustments during the first years of marriage. When a couple shares the same religious affiliation, their divorce probability within the first four years of marriage is twenty percent lower than it would be if they had different religious beliefs.[34]

Faith awakening in new parents

The children born of your marriage are a principal reason why you want to have a shared faith. Children dramatically change the equation in mixed-faith households. The divorce rate of mixed-faith couples *with children* is three times higher than in same-faith households.[35]

To their surprise, many couples have a faith-awakening experience after the birth of their first child. Before becoming parents, your different faiths may not seem like a big deal. Suddenly, you're filled with questions: "Will the baby be baptized?" "In which church will the baby be baptized?" "Where will the child be catechized?" And out of nowhere, you start getting some phone calls from in-laws expressing strong opinions on what should be done.

Faced with such questions, some interfaith couples experience division at a moment when they most need unity. Other interfaith couples try to preserve unity by "agreeing to disagree" about faith questions, or they just drop out of church life altogether. They may even say, "We'll let the child decide when he becomes an adult." Yet even when a husband and wife themselves find equilibrium in an interfaith marriage, a child is liable to be confused or even torn apart by divided loyalties.

Why take the risk?

The conflicts outlined above are merely potential clashes. They don't automatically occur in interfaith marriages. Many interfaith couples successfully navigate between these differences without marital discord. But again, why take the risk, especially if your faith is the most meaningful part of your life? Why not marry someone who shares your faith in order to guarantee that you'll at least start your marriage with a common outlook?

God is the best friend that marriage ever had. Don't run the risk of leaving Him out. It's well worth waiting for a woman who shares your faith.

CHAPTER TEN

J

Just How Far Can We Go?

For everything there is a season, and a time for every matter under heaven . . . a time to embrace, and a time to refrain from embracing" (Ecclesiastes 3:1, 5).

"Okay," you may say, "I'm with you that sexual relations should wait for marriage, as you described in chapter 3. But in the meantime, just how far can we go while waiting for marriage? Aren't kissing and petting okay?"

The marital embrace is a consuming fire

To answer the kissing and petting question, you need to consider how God designed the marital embrace, along with all the acts leading up to it. He created sex in marriage to be a consuming fire in two respects. First, He made the wonderful flame of the marital embrace itself—a flame that can burn for decades without losing its warmth. Second, once the fire of physical love is intentionally ignited, He's designed it to increase in intensity, until it's fully consummated in the marital embrace.

If you say that you and your girlfriend can fire up steamy passions over an extended period of time and never have problems with serious sexual temptations, then may I suggest a visit to a physician or psychiatrist? Intimate kissing and caressing are designed to ignite the flames of marital love between husband and wife. In creating the great mystery of the marital embrace, God hasn't designed any convenient stopping points on the way to consummated physical love.

An exhortation from the world's best love song

In the Old Testament, the Song of Songs (also called the Song of Solomon) is an extended love song. The Hebrew title means that it's the greatest of songs. Using the poetic imagery of the passionate love between spouses newly joined in the marriage covenant, the book subtly describes the love between God and His covenant people. The poetic imagery is rich, and much can be gleaned from it.

If you want the best answer to the kissing and caressing question, then listen to the advice at the close of the world's greatest love song: "I adjure you . . . that you stir not up nor awaken love until it please. For love is strong as death. Its flashes are flashes of fire, a most vehement flame. Many waters cannot quench love, neither can floods drown it" (Song of Songs 8:4, 6–7).

Marital love is something profound, powerful, all-consuming, and sacred. God intended it to consume a man and a woman entirely in the marital embrace. Don't run the risk of stirring it up before marriage.

Men and sexual temptation

When I have talked with men about the "hands off–no kissing sessions" recommendation, they usually say at first that this advice goes way too far. Yet when confronted with the fact that they and most of their friends have struggled with going too far after some innocent kissing and hugging, they end up admitting that this advice isn't so much radical as it is realistic.

Many women fail to appreciate how easily a man can be aroused. A woman may say to herself, "There's no harm in a little kissing," not realizing that this simple physical stimulus, while it may be morally permissible, may also be enough to awaken a strong desire for full sexual expression in a man. The time of kissing ends up either going too far or leaving the man feeling defrauded. Neither of these options is an expression of true love.

Erosion of moral standards

There is an ever-present temptation for chastity educators to "baptize" the previous stage of our culture's slide toward Gomorrah. Some of the advice in this chapter has been criticized—by some who apparently do not read older books on this subject. Respected moral theologians of just a generation ago taught that just keeping steady company with a person of the opposite sex when there was no immediate prospect for marriage was a proximate occasion of sin.

Avoiding regrets

Some people enjoy playing with fire, convinced that they'll never be burned. Yet millions (yes, millions!) of Christian couples intending to remain chaste until marriage have fallen into sexual sin that began with the spark of a little "innocent" kissing. These couples deeply regret that they ever started expressing physical affection before marriage. So why take the risk, especially if you really love someone?

If you deeply love a woman and hope to marry her, then you don't want your physical affection to get out of control. Unfortunately, the only way many couples can check their physical desires is to break off the relationship. That's why premarital sex has prematurely ended countless Christian relationships.

Relationship insurance

Postponing all physical affection until marriage is insurance for a relationship that you really care about. The wisest answer to the "Just how far can we go?" question is simply "Zero," "*Nada*," "Zip." Save *all* the fire for your marriage, and your relationship won't get burned. Guaranteed.

Shortly after I met my wife, Karen, I knew she was someone I was *really* interested in. I wanted our friendship to grow without getting out of hand. So that she didn't think my lack of physical advances stemmed from a lack of interest in her, I suggested that we postpone all physical affection to preserve our special relationship. We never kissed until after she accepted my proposal for marriage.

I thought our waiting to kiss until we were engaged was really radical back in 1978. But today there are Christian couples who are taking their relationship insurance a step further. They're holding off their first kiss until they're declared to be "man and wife."[36] I guarantee that you'll never regret such a wait.

If you need convincing, take a look at the smiling faces and sparkling eyes of the couples who waited for their first kiss at the altar. Instead of fizzling out after a few years, the fires of marital love are blazing in these formerly courting couples. Who would want anything less?

Help for maintaining your standards

If you agree that kissing and hugging sessions are off-limits until marriage, you might still wonder, "Where can we find help and encouragement for keeping our commitment?" I repeat my earlier suggestion: Find a "mentoring couple" (see chapter 4) to assist you. An ideal mentoring couple is a husband and wife with a solid marriage who are willing to meet with the two of you at least monthly.

With the increased temptations to intimacy that arise during engagement, you'll probably want to meet weekly, or biweekly, once you're engaged. A wise engaged couple will take this precautionary step to ensure that the first full expression of sexual love is not in sin, but in the sacredness of marital love. Your mentoring couple will help hold you accountable to your standards during courtship and engagement.

If you set the standard of no sexual expression until marriage, then the mentoring couple asks you at each meeting if you've lived up to that standard. It may be just that little bit of help you need to stick to your standards. Like a weekly Weight Watchers meeting where your friends see you step on the scale, accountability helps you pass up tempting choices.

Short-circuited decision making

There's one final reason why you don't want to arouse your passions before marriage. Deciding to marry someone is the greatest decision you'll make in life. No other decision requires such prudent, prayerful, and careful thinking. At no other time in life is it so important that you keep yourself levelheaded.

If you overload your emotions with flaming physical passion, your brain's decision-making process will be short-circuited. Rational thought will fly out the window as your passions rule, and the likelihood of making a regrettable marital decision is magnified. You can't be sure of keeping your head if you're involved physically. You could easily be led by your feelings into a lifelong commitment that you may seriously regret.

No wonder St. Paul gave such a stern warning against choosing a spouse in the passions of lust:

"For you know what instructions we gave you through the Lord Jesus. For this is the will of God, your sanctification: that you abstain from immorality; that each one of you know how to control his own body in holiness and honor, not in the passion of lust like heathen who do not know God; that no man transgress, and wrong his brother in this matter, because the Lord is an avenger in all these things, as we solemnly forewarned you" (1 Thessalonians 4:2–6).

You really don't want to have your emotions set on fire with the passion of lust when you're about to make the greatest decision of your life. Don't stir up or awaken physical intimacy until you're married. Once you're married, then you can light that "most vehement flame" of marital love—a love that time will not extinguish.

CHAPTER ELEVEN

K

Know Yourself and Your Future Mate

S he's charming, witty, really good-looking, and seems agreeable on most everything. To top it all off, she loves you. What else could you possibly need to know?

Lots! The adage "Marry in haste, repent at leisure," is still true in the twenty-first century. An adrenaline rush to the altar is foolish. Haste to get married is usually infatuation and certainly not genuine love.

While recreational dating lacks any definite aim, the specific purpose of courting is to get to know a woman well enough to make a wise choice about marrying her. A prudent decision is made with as much information as possible about yourself and your future mate.

Gain valuable insights from the family circle

The discernment process begins in your family and in her family. As we've already noted, the imprudent dating patterns of the twentieth century removed courtship from the family circle, with tragic consequences. Wise men will seek their parents' guidance and blessing in each of the various stages in the selection of a marriage partner.

You're shortchanging yourself if you simply bring a prospective mate home for the weekend, announce your engagement, and ask your parents to rubber-stamp your wedding plans. Many heart-wrenching marital mistakes could be avoided if men would enlist their family's aid to gain an honest assessment of the women they're interested in.

One of the unique benefits your family can offer is that they really know you. To make a good marital choice you need to know both yourself and your prospective mate. Often, your family will see things about your relationship that you can't immediately perceive. Be open and attentive to their observations, suggestions, and comments. Allow your family abundant time to get to know the woman you're courting.

Likewise, getting to know her parents, siblings, and grandparents will give you insights into the woman you're interested in. The generous amount of time you spend with her family, and she with yours, is vital in deciding whether or not to marry.

Value of marriage preparation

In addition, church-based marriage preparation classes and competent premarital counseling programs can provide valuable assistance in making a good marriage choice. Rather than viewing such programs as obstacles to be overcome on the way to the altar, you should appreciate and eagerly participate in them. Solid marriage preparation classes have demonstrated a wonderful ability to strengthen marriages and lower the probability of divorce.

Such classes will assist you in really getting to know each other. Marital preparation classes will give you penetrating questions to ask each other—questions that you may never have thought to ask. I suggest that you don't publicly announce a wedding date until you've completed *at least* half a marital preparation program.

Discern before deciding

You want to know as much as possible about yourself and your future mate before making the greatest decision in your life.[37] You want to know as much as you can about her character, religious commitment, disposition, personality type, employment and educational background, health status, and family background. You need to consider if there are any previous marriages; any dependents; present or past addictions; criminal records; credit problems or bankruptcies; psychological or health problems; or abusive situations in either of your family backgrounds.

You can avoid these topics, or easily hide them during engagement, but believe me: They will surface in marriage. A good counselor can help the two of you openly discuss and deal with such sensitive issues. Some of these questions take only a few minutes to cover with a counselor, but tackling these topics can prevent decades of unimaginable heartache.

Avoid my mistake

I need to tell you about a big mistake I've made in the past when providing premarital counseling. I thought it was sufficient to receive an open acknowledgement of potential problems from a couple after pointing out obvious areas of possible conflict and incompatibility. But I was wrong—in some cases, tragically wrong.

Simply recognizing and admitting a potential source of serious marital conflict is useless unless meaningful action is taken to change it. I naively imagined that an acknowledgement, joined by a serious pledge "to work on it," was enough. But subsequent unhappiness, marital strife, and divorce in the lives of some couples I'd counseled showed me that this wasn't enough. Real action with substantial evidence of improvement *before* marriage was needed. Why risk entering into marriage unless significant change has already taken place and potentially serious sources of marital strife have been removed?

What you see is what you get

As the president of a non-profit organization, I've had to learn an important principle for good hiring that you can use in choosing a wife as well. I've found that in ninety-nine percent of employment decisions, "What You See Is What You Get" (WYSIWYG).

As an employer, I've made the mistake of imagining that an employee would function as I would if I were in that particular position. But people are very likely to function in a new position much as they have functioned in the past, especially in the recent past. I've had to curb my personal projections about what a person *might* do, and instead carefully observe what he was *actually* doing.

The same is true in choosing a wife: You need to see how she is now in real life, not how you imagine her to be in a blissful romantic fantasy of a future marriage. If you really don't like what you see now, then don't marry the woman.

Don't think that a wedding ceremony followed by a few months of marriage will change your wife into your imaginary image of a great wife. Personality traits, levels of motivation, personal and family habits, character, interests, temperament, and life priorities are not magically transformed by walking down an aisle. Remember WYSIWYG!

No, you don't have to find Ms. Perfect. She doesn't exist, and you don't have the right to demand perfection unless you happen to fall into that category yourself. But you should have a clear idea of who it is you're marrying, and especially take note of any character defects you would find impossible to live with. If you've done your homework, then you'll never have to lament, "Oh, if only I had known."

The time for commitment

If, after a sufficient time to get to know each other's character, disposition, and background, you like what you've learned, and if you've obtained good premarital counseling and your parents' blessings, then go ahead and make your decision. There's no need to prolong your engagement unduly after this point without a strong, mutually-agreed-upon reason to do so. Just go into marriage with your eyes wide open.

CHAPTER TWELVE

L

Love is Blind—but Premarital Inventories Aid Sight Recovery

Infatuation and purely emotional love may be blind, but you shouldn't be. Be sure to utilize resources that will help give you 20/20 vision before deciding upon a life partner.

Premarital inventories, especially the ones known as PREPARE and FOCCUS, have stunning track records in predicting the probabilities of marital success or failure. While these inventories resist describing themselves as predictive instruments, both FOCCUS and PREPARE have high levels of reliability verified through third-party follow-up studies. They are among the best of the premarital inventories. FOCCUS was found to predict high-quality versus low-quality relationships with eighty percent to eighty-two percent reliability. PREPARE has demonstrated an ability to distinguish couples who eventually get divorced from those who remain happily married, with eighty percent to eighty-five percent accuracy.

These are astonishing results. If you're serious about getting assistance in discerning a potentially high-risk relationship, or a potentially successful one, then the modest amount of time and money required for an assessment such as FOCCUS or PREPARE is a smart investment in your future.

One strong caution about exaggerated expectations from these inventories: Sometimes unwarranted assumptions and excessive dependencies are attributed to them. These inventories are *not* pass-or-fail tests. They don't make any claim to give an infallible prediction about any single relationship. A premarital inventory should not be used as the sole criterion in making a marriage decision.

The purpose of premarital inventories is to point out areas of both strength and challenge. Their special value extends far beyond the actual assessment, especially in the way they often spark deeper levels of communication, problem-solving, and clear-headed thinking. Using a premarital inventory can help you start talking about some topics that you may have been avoiding. Inventories cover areas such as finances, role relations, in-laws, leisure, sex, communication, and conflict resolution.

FOCCUS
Facilitating Open Couple Communication, Understanding, and Study

3214 N. 60th St., Omaha, NE 68104;
1-888-874-2684; www.foccusinc.com

FOCCUS was developed by experienced marriage and family counselors through the Family Life Office in Omaha, Nebraska. FOCCUS, while covering the same wide range of topics as other inventories, includes an important spiritual component. Since studies show that couples with a strong faith life in their marriages are more stable and satisfied in their relationships, it makes lots of sense to include spirituality in a premarital inventory—especially for Christians. FOCCUS is offered in four editions, including a Christian non-denominational edition and a Catholic edition.

FOCCUS, like PREPARE, can be used for those seriously considering marriage as well as those who are already engaged. (There is also a REFOCCUS marital inventory available to couples wishing to improve their relationship in their existing marriage.)

FOCCUS is very affordable. I can't think of a single reason why every about-to-be-engaged, or already-engaged, couple would not want to take the FOCCUS inventory.

PREPARE

P.O. Box 190, Minneapolis, MN 55440;
1-800-331-1661; www.prepare-enrich.com

More than a million couples have taken PREPARE (for premarital couples) and ENRICH (for married couples). The inventory's goal is to assess and explore your relationship's strengths as well as areas needing growth. Couples take a 195-question inventory to help prepare them for marriage and to enrich their relationship.

The PREPARE inventory, like FOCCUS, has high levels of reliability, verified through follow-up studies. PREPARE offers excellent materials for couples as a way of following up on the discoveries made when taking the inventory. Either one of these inventories will provide a valuable assessment of your relationship.

Remember, these inventories do not and cannot make any marital decision for you. Their value is in giving you a clearer picture of your relationship, and based on that, *you* can make a better-informed decision.

My only criticism of PREPARE and FOCCUS is that they are priced too economically. I'm afraid that their low price might suggest a low worth to some couples. I'd still recommend these instruments even if they cost as much as a wedding cake. When you consider that they cost only a tiny fraction of what most couples spend on their cake, there's no excuse for not taking advantage of them.

This may not be earth-shaking news to you, but many men aren't excited about going to premarital classes. Yet follow-up studies of premarital classes have reported that men like the inventories better than any other part of the classes. Tuck this fact away in case you feel tempted to drag your heels over taking a premarital inventory in a marriage preparation class.

Premarital inventories accelerate relationships

Taking one of these inventories is an eye-opening experience for couples contemplating marriage. The process will either accelerate the development of your relationship or accelerate its breakup. About ten percent of those taking PREPARE or a similar inventory end up postponing or breaking off their engagement, or even ending their relationship.

You might react to this statistic by saying, "I don't want anything to do with these things!" or asking, "Why should I jeopardize my engagement?" The answer is twofold.

First, while these instruments result in some couples breaking off their engagement, many others find their relationships greatly strengthened because they go on to explore the findings of the inventories with each other and with a counselor.

Second, you don't need to take a blind leap to enter marriage. Many young people are avoiding marriage altogether because they're scared of falling into an ocean of divorce-inflicted heartbreaks. These instruments will help you see what you're getting into. Again, they don't give any absolute guarantee, but they can certainly help you know yourself and your potential spouse more accurately.

Your decision comes before setting the date

Never announce a wedding date before fully determining whether a particular woman should be your mate. Prematurely setting a wedding date shuts down the decision-making process and sets you up for getting pressured into a marriage you may feel uncomfortable about.

Before announcing a wedding date, you need competent counsel from your family, your church, or marriage counselors. I personally refuse to start premarital counseling with couples who have announced a wedding date. Once the date is set and announced, the big decision about whom to marry is eclipsed by decisions about bridesmaids, dresses, florists, photographers, cake, invitations, and a thousand other concerns.

While many couples regard joining a premarital program as a certain step toward marriage, you should consider the final decision an open question until you've completed at least half a premarital program and have taken either the FOCCUS or PREPARE inventories.

Special step before engagement

I am a big fan of premarital inventories, but their one major flaw is that they are normally used *after* engagement. Time spent together, growing affection, and the dramatically increased bonding that comes with engagement accelerates the relationship building and bonding process. Your relationship at this stage is like a runaway train whose momentum is taking you down the aisle.

Even if your premarital inventory turns up significant warning signals, will you find the willpower to apply the brakes? Some couples do, but many others don't. Also, wouldn't it be much fairer to break a courtship rather than an engagement because of what you learn from taking a premarital inventory earlier in your relationship?

During the pre-engagement phase of your relationship, I recommend a fast, effective, and economical premarital online inventory called RELATE. This premarital instrument gives couples an immediate detailed report on themselves and their relationship. The report includes graphs, charts, and guidelines for interpretation of the results, allowing couples to recognize their strengths and identify potential problems. It is a good aid in helping you see whether your relationship has the necessary ingredients to stand the test of time.

Information about RELATE can be found online at: http://relate.byu.edu.

This simple step with RELATE will provide a valuable assessment of your relationship *before* making a decision to get engaged. To deepen your relationship after engagement, I still recommend using either PREPARE or FOCCUS with a counselor during your premarital classes and sessions.

The decision whom to marry is one of the most important you will ever make. The premarital inventories will assist you in making a wiser marriage decision. Take your close look now. Then, once you're married, you'll never need to look back.

CHAPTER THIRTEEN

M

Marriage is a Sacrament—a Mystery of Grace and Love

A re you interested in discovering some astonishingly good news about marriage? If your answer is yes, then I suggest that you read this chapter slowly and carefully.

The Trinity and the sacrament of marriage

At the heart of the universe is the Blessed Trinity. A fire of divine love radiates between the three Persons of the Trinity. The intensity of this divine love burns brighter than the sun. The *Catechism* says: "The mystery of the Most Holy Trinity is the central mystery of Christian faith and life. It is the mystery of God in Himself. It is therefore the source of all the other mysteries of faith, the light that enlightens them."[38]

The Trinity holds the secret to the depths of love possible in the sacrament of marriage. You were made to know and experience the love of God. Your greatest destiny is to be joined to Him as an adopted son of the Blessed Trinity. By baptism in Christ, you were joined in a family bond, a covenant, with God as your Father, with Jesus as your covenant Brother, and with the Holy Spirit.

When a baptized man and a baptized woman with their free consent bind themselves together for life in a lawful marriage, they enter the sacrament of matrimony. The *Baltimore Catechism* defines a sacrament as "an outward sign instituted by Christ to give grace." This grace unites us to Christ and the entire Trinity in a covenant bond of love.

The fire of divine love in your marriage

The flame of divine love within the Blessed Trinity is imparted in a special way to a man and a woman joined in the sacrament of marriage. As Moses was told to remove his shoes before the burning bush because he was standing on holy ground, so with reverence are we to regard the sacrament of marriage as a holy and sacred dwelling where the fires of divine charity burn.

God is willing to enkindle the deepest of affections between you and your future wife in the sacrament of marriage. The fire of divine charity from within the heart of the universe, the Blessed Trinity, can be in your heart, your wife's heart, and in the heart of your marriage.

St. Paul says that the very love with which Christ loves the Church is mysteriously present in the New Covenant sacrament of marriage (see Ephesians 5:25–33). In the New Covenant, Christ has elevated the good of natural marriage to incredible heights. He made matrimony a sacrament, and He has taken marriage into Himself.

A husband's heartfelt affection

How might this vision of the sacrament of marriage be expressed to your future wife? St. John Chrysostom, commenting on Ephesians 5, suggests that young Christian husbands should say to their wives: "I have taken you in my arms, and I love you, and I prefer you to my life itself. For the present life is nothing, and my most ardent dream is to spend it with you in such a way that we may be assured of not being separated in the life reserved for us . . . I place your love above all things."[39]

Families as reflections of the Trinity

Art and icons have captured the sublime greatness of the Christian family by depicting the Holy Family (Jesus, Mary, and Joseph) as an earthly reflection of the familial relations within the Trinity. Just like the Holy Family, every Christian family's calling is to reflect the mystery of Trinitarian life.

What does this hold for you as a future Christian husband and father? It means that you, like St. Joseph, will be a reflection of the Heavenly Father to your family. Pope John Paul II has said that the heart of fatherhood consists "in revealing and in reliving on earth the very fatherhood of God."[40] If you are like most men, you love a real challenge. What a staggering challenge—and responsibility—is the call to Christian marriage and fatherhood!

What happened to marriage?

What in the world has happened to marriage? Instead of this exalted view of a marvelous Christian sacrament, we're more likely to see marriages resembling a defective booster rocket: They fire up, blast off, spin out of control, and land not long afterwards with a crash and burn.

Many reasons can be given for the current pitiful state of marriage and family life, but one particular reason is generally neglected by social scientists. Around the time of the Protestant Reformation, Christian marriage was explicitly denied by the Reformers to be a sacrament. They still held it to be an important divine institution, but they unfortunately declared that it was essentially a civil union.

With the rapid rise of many of the new nation-states, primary jurisdiction over marriage was transferred from Church to state, and marriage itself was devalued from a sacrament to a civil contract.[41] It took a few hundred years for the effects of this switch to work their way into society. But today we see the ripe fruits of the change in drive-through weddings, instant no-fault divorces, and soaring divorce rates—even among Christians.

The ultimate renewal of marriage

Many noble and well-intentioned efforts are underway today to reform civil marriage. Such efforts, while commendable, can only go so far. Marriage as a civil institution is essentially a breakable contract. In the near future, the state will probably view marriage as a breakable contract simply between two persons, not necessarily between a man and a woman. While we assuredly can reduce a good deal of the runaway rate of marital breakup through civil reforms, we cannot really heal the heart of Christian marriage without a conscious return to the sacrament of marriage.

So what will you do? I can't imagine a Christian of any denominational background reading this chapter and not wanting to experience all the sacramental blessings of marriage. You and your future wife will want to enter marriage with a full conviction that it's a sacrament. To bolster your understanding, I encourage reading (and meditating) on the subject of marriage from Christian traditions that have continuously honored it as a sacrament. A reliable and readable introduction to the sacrament of marriage can be found in the *Catechism of the Catholic Church* (paragraphs 1601–1666).

The civil government can give you a marriage certificate, and a divorce later on if things don't go well. Christ, by elevating marriage to a sacrament, can give you and your future spouse special, long-lasting marital graces that will inflame your covenant union with divine love.

An often overlooked resource for the sacrament of marriage

Pope Pius XI, describing the graces available in the sacrament of marriage, had this to say:

> The grace of matrimony will remain for the most part an unused talent hidden in the field unless the parties exercise these supernatural powers and cultivate and develop the seeds of grace they have received. If, however, doing all that lies within their power, they cooperate diligently, they will be able with ease to bear the burdens of their state and to fulfill their duties.
>
> An oft-repeated consideration of their state of life, and a diligent reflection on the sacrament they have received, will be of great assistance to them. Let them constantly keep in mind, that they have been sanctified and strengthened for the duties and for the dignity of their state by a special sacrament, the efficacious power of which . . . is undying.

> Let not, then, those who are joined in matrimony neglect the grace of the sacrament which is in them.[42]

For lasting love you'll need a constant source of strength invigorating your marriage. For those Christian couples who are careful to appropriate them, the sacramental graces of matrimony bring the fires of divine love from the Blessed Trinity into the heart of their marriage. This is one treasure you don't want to neglect in your marriage. Why not start now to develop your appreciation and understanding of the sacrament of marriage?

CHAPTER FOURTEEN

N

Narcissistic Women

The very last person you want to select as a wife is a narcissistic woman. The self-centered, self-absorbed, and self-admiring woman is searching for a husband to orbit her over-sized ego, and you don't want to be that man.

Women in love with themselves

Why do men so often fall for women stuck on themselves? It's easy to understand why a man would be attracted to a woman with good looks and above-average intelligence. Yet these are the types of women most prone to fall in love with themselves.

Women of humble circumstances are certainly liable to self-love. But women blessed with an exceptional amount of beauty, brains, or wealth are easy prey in the clutches of narcissism. Even if a narcissistic woman is loaded with good looks, smarts, or money, unhappiness waits for the man foolish enough to marry her.

As we noted before, the Bible warns: "Like a gold ring in a swine's snout is a beautiful woman without discretion" (Proverbs 11:2). Mentally visualize this verse if you're ever tempted to fall for a gorgeous woman without inner beauty. It is worth waiting for a woman with the hidden beauty of the heart.

Greater gifts require greater grace

If you're considering marriage to a woman with great gifts, then make sure she avails herself of greater measures of grace. The book of Sirach says, "The greater you are, the more you must humble yourself; so you will find favor in the sight of the Lord" (3:18).

Women deprived of stable family life and two loving parents may also be prone to excessive self-love. The early years of family life are critical in helping a person mature beyond childish self-centeredness into an adulthood capable of self-giving love. A dysfunctional family environment can arrest this process of maturation.

I'm not implying here that every young woman from a dysfunctional family, or who is exceptionally talented or good-looking, will be narcissistic. You just need to keep your personal "radar warning system" functioning so you can avoid getting entangled with someone who's orbiting around her ego. Obsessions with showy clothes, expensive jewelry, and heavy cosmetics may warn of a woman's narcissistic thirst for attention. Don't allow yourself to become attracted to glittery outward adornment disguising a narcissistic heart.

Determining what lies at the core of a woman

St. Augustine said in his book *The City of God* that humanity is divided into two "cities." The first "city," the city of the world, is fixated on a love of self. This is the condition of people unchanged by God's saving grace in Christ. In contrast is the second "city," the city of God, characterized by a love for both God and neighbor.

While everyone struggles with a tendency toward self-centeredness, some people have enthroned their own egos in their hearts. So you need to determine what lies at the core of the woman you're interested in. Does she live in the city of the world or the city of God? Is her fundamental life-orientation self-centered or God-centered?

If selfishness rules her, she won't be able to offer self-giving love in marriage—unless she has a spiritual conversion. A new life in Christ entails a death to our old ego and a rebirth with Christ living, reigning, and loving from the center of our life. St. Paul described this ego transformation in his own life this way: "I have been crucified with Christ; it is no longer I who live, but Christ who lives in me; and the life I now live in the flesh I live by faith in the Son of God, who loved me and gave himself for me" (Galatians 2:20).

Married life can be marvelous or miserable, depending upon your choice of a wife. A woman transformed by grace, who loves God and neighbor, is the kind of woman you want pledging lifelong love to you.

CHAPTER FIFTEEN

O

Occasional Fights Are Okay—*Really!*

You and your fiancée just had a big blowup, so now you're thinking about breaking off your engagement. With profound disillusionment you're saying to yourself, "If two people really loved each other, they would never have a fight like we had."

Slow down. A fight doesn't necessarily mean you should break an engagement or end a relationship.

Targeting problems rather than each other

If you've had a fight and were able to identify and target the problem causing friction between the two of you, rather than just blasting each other, then you're far better prepared for a lasting marriage than a couple who has never fought. So don't break off your engagement just because you had a heated argument. What you do need is to learn conflict resolution skills to deal with the inevitable differences that arise in marriage.

You need to know three facts about marital and premarital fights. First, *all* married couples fight, even though many couples fail to admit it. At a recent conference for Christian husbands and fathers, I asked the two hundred men in attendance, "How many of you have fights with your wife?" About a dozen men raised their hands. I told the rest of the men that they might need to go to confession for being less than truthful.

The number-one predictor of divorce

Second, just because you fight doesn't mean that your marriage will be doomed. In fact, the opposite may be true. Secular marriage research has found that the habitual *avoidance* of conflict is the number-one predictor of divorce. Amazingly, the couples who stay married don't have fewer differences or fights than couples who divorce. Both sets of couples disagree about the same types of things (money, kids, sexual relations, housework, in-laws). The big difference between the two groups of couples is *how* they handle their disagreements. For instance, constant criticism, contempt, biting sarcasm, and stonewalling during arguments are high predictors of divorce.

Taming the tongue

Third, remember that a great way to prevent conflicts, or to heal ones already underway, is to tame the tongue. Jesus taught us to pray: "Lead us not into temptation" (Matthew 6:13). Since the tongue so often leads the way into discord, it's wise for every Christian couple to pray daily for control of the tongue. The words of Psalm 19:14 form a short yet effective prayer for control of the tongue: "Let the words of my mouth and the meditation of my heart be acceptable in thy sight, O LORD, my rock and my redeemer."

If an argument erupts, but it's still in the early "flaring up" stage, remember a couple of verses from Proverbs that can come to your rescue:

"A soft answer turns away wrath, but a harsh word stirs up anger" (Proverbs 15:1).

"There is one whose rash words are like sword thrusts, but the tongue of the wise brings healing" (Proverbs 12:18).

If you do find yourself flaming mad during an argument, then realize that a man's physiological reactions during an argument are different from a woman's. A verbal or physical conflict triggers a man's fighting instinct, causing an adrenaline rush. While your fiancée may be immediately ready to talk things out, your body needs twenty minutes for your adrenaline to calm before a rational discussion. Just let her know you need a few minutes to cool down.

Learn how to fight *for* your marriage

Consistent marital research shows that how spouses communicate when trying to resolve a marital conflict predicts marital satisfaction and the probability of divorce. Without the skills to resolve their conflicts, it's usually just a question of time until problems accumulate or escalate, eroding marital satisfaction.[43] The sooner you and your fiancée learn these skills the better.

PREP (Prevention and Relationship Enhancement Program) is probably the most effective marriage communication enhancement program. It provides training to teach you how to fight fairly for your marriage. It will teach you simple ways to handle engagement and marital differences without destroying your relationship.

PREP has demonstrated effectiveness in preventing divorce and reducing strains in stressed marriages. In research funded by the National Institute of Mental Health, PREP couples had one-third the break-up rate of control couples after five years.

PREP is designed for both engaged couples and already married couples. There is a recommended Christian version of PREP. To find a schedule for PREP training, go to their Web site.[44] I can't think of a more valuable present for an engaged or newly married couple than sponsorship to a Christian PREP training weekend.

You don't need to be leery of PREP's communication training. PREP does not require you to "spill your guts" in psychobabble encounter groups. Instead, this is skill-based training. Just as in baseball you need to learn how to hit, throw, catch, run, and slide, so for your successful engagement and marriage you need to learn communication skills.

Real married life, engagements, courtships, and even honeymoons have occasional fights. Such times, though trying, aren't signs of the end of your relationship. They are actually opportunities for deepening your love and strengthening your communication—especially if you have learned the basic skills for resolving conflicts.

CHAPTER SIXTEEN

P

Pray for a Good Wife

D ave, a senior at the Franciscan University of Steubenville, Ohio, sensed that the time was right to begin seeking a wife. He went to the campus chapel and prayed in the presence of the Blessed Sacrament for a life partner. Just then, Trina, also a senior, decided to make a prayer visit to the chapel on her way from the library back to her dorm.

As Dave was leaving the chapel, he met Trina. Although they had seen each other on campus, this was the first time they had really met and stopped to talk. I'm sure Dave wasn't expecting such a quick answer to his prayers for a wife, but that's what happened. Dave and Trina were married eighteen months later. They are now the parents of a beautiful little girl and a handsome son.

We can reverently pray anywhere, at anytime, and expect God to hear our prayer. Yet St. John's Gospel clearly indicates a special context for effectual prayer. In the very process of instituting the Blessed Sacrament during the Last

Supper, Jesus said: "Whatever you ask in my name, I will do it, that the Father may be glorified in the Son; if you ask anything in my name, I will do it" (John 14:13–14). A special dynamism takes place when you present your prayer requests for a good wife to God the Father in the name of Jesus while in the presence of the Blessed Sacrament (see also John 15:7, 16:23–24).

Jesus taught us to pray for *all* our needs, not just those items we might regard as "spiritual." For instance, in the "Our Father," Jesus taught us to pray to our heavenly Father for things as basic as daily bread. Certainly, then, praying for a good Christian wife should not be outside the scope of your prayer life.

Proverbs says, "House and wealth are inherited from fathers, but a prudent wife is from the LORD" (Proverbs 19:14). Prayer for a spouse is a primary way we exercise our dependency upon God for a good wife.

Don't fear being honest with God when praying for a spouse. He already knows the deepest thoughts and desires of your heart. If you're anxious about finding a mate, then "cast all your anxieties on Him, for He cares about you" (1 Peter 5:7).

Turning cares into prayers

It's wisely said that the best cure for anxiety is to turn your cares into prayers. St. Paul insisted: "Have no anxiety about anything, but in everything by prayer and supplication with thanksgiving let your requests be made known to God. And the peace of God, which passes all understanding, will keep your hearts and your minds in Christ Jesus" (Philippians 4:6–7).

Since you are to pray "Thy will be done," you should ask God to reveal His will for a spouse. Ask Jesus, the Good

Shepherd, to direct your steps in fulfilling His will. Keep before you Scripture verses for guidance such as these:

"Trust in the LORD with all your heart, and do not rely on your own insight. In all your ways acknowledge Him, and He will make straight your paths" (Proverbs 3:5–6).

"Teach me to do Thy will, for Thou art my God! Let Thy good spirit lead me on a level path" (Psalm 143:10).

Just in case someone reading this book needs to hear this admonition, I should note that horoscopes are highly displeasing to God and are a sinful way to seek guidance. Turning to horoscopes is turning away from trust in God.

Lead us not into disastrous decisions

Prayer for guidance also means asking for God's help in not being led into temptation. Ask God to keep you from making a catastrophic decision. Ask for protective guidance from your guardian angel and from St. Raphael.

The archangel Raphael in the Old Testament book of Tobit disguised himself as a traveling companion of Tobias. (The book of Tobit is not found in Protestant Bibles, but it's in the Septuagint, the Greek edition of the Old Testament used by St. Paul and the early Church, and it's been in the Catholic Bible ever since.) St. Raphael provided protection and guidance for Tobias on his way to meet and marry Sarah. You too should ask for the assistance of this archangel, who is the patron of engaged couples.

Pray for your future wife

Right now, you can start praying for your future wife. Even though you may have no idea who your wife will be, God certainly knows. A good Christian friend of mine, J. P., told me that he credits his avoiding the many moral pitfalls in college and in the military to the prayers of his wife, Louise, long before they even met. J. P. looked me in the eye and said, "Where I am today as a Christian is because of her prayers for me before we ever came together." Starting today, you can pray for your future wife's growth in Christian maturity, her angelic protection, and her divine guidance.

Asking the Holy Family to pray for you

The Bible says, "The prayer of a righteous man [or woman] has great power in its effects" (James 5:16). Certainly, Mary, Jesus' mother, and Joseph, the foster-father of Jesus, are the righteous saints closest to Jesus who can intercede with their Son on your behalf. In fact, you should seek the prayer assistance of the entire Holy Family (Jesus, Mary, and Joseph) as you seek to start your family.

When you pray, ask for a few ounces of patience. Patience allows us to avoid panicking about a spouse and settling for second best. Wait for God to give you the incomparable gift of a good spouse.

A love story from Genesis

One of the greatest marriage stories in the Bible is that of Isaac and Rebekah in Genesis, chapter 24. The patriarch Abraham, an earthly reflection of the heavenly Father, sends his servant (an image of the Holy Spirit) to a distant country to find and bring a bride home to his son Isaac. Through a series of providential events, the servant meets Rebekah and is introduced to her family. Rebekah, with her family's blessing, consents to go with the servant to marry Isaac.

Trusting in his father's efforts to provide a good bride, Isaac was back home contentedly watching the flock. One evening Isaac went out into the field to meditate. Just then the servant and Rebekah approached from a distance.

What would this first meeting be like? Would Rebekah be disappointed in the man that Divine Providence was leading her to? Would Isaac reject his father's choice of a bride? Not at all!

The Bible says, "Rebekah lifted up her eyes, and when she saw Isaac, she alighted from the camel, and said to the servant, 'Who is the man yonder, walking in the field to meet us?' The servant said, 'It is my master'" (Genesis 24:64–65). Isaac and Rebekah had been destined for each other, yet only now would they have the thrill of meeting.

I've had one unforgettable experience of riding a camel, and it seems to me that a person would have to be highly excited to "alight from a camel." Rebekah was obviously taken when she saw Isaac, the man God had prepared for her. Isaac graciously received Rebekah as his wife and loved her.[45]

The Bible says, "Take delight in the Lord, and He will give you the desires of your heart" (Psalm 37:4). You can trust God, as Isaac did, to give you the desires of your heart.

A secret to divine guidance

You should keep in mind this secret to divine guidance: I've found that God's gracious hand often acts after we've served others. Isaiah chapter 58 is the clearest Scripture passage teaching this principle:

> Is not this the fast that I choose: to loose the
> bonds of wickedness, to undo the thongs of

the yoke, to let the oppressed go free, and to break every yoke? Is it not to share your bread with the hungry, and bring the homeless poor into your house; when you see the naked, to cover him, and not to hide yourself from your own flesh? **Then shall your light break forth like the dawn**, and your healing shall spring up speedily; your righteousness shall go before you, the glory of the LORD shall be your rear guard. **Then you shall call, and the LORD will answer; you shall cry, and He will say, Here I am . . .** If you pour yourself out for the hungry and satisfy the desire of the afflicted, then shall your light rise in the darkness and your gloom be as the noonday. **And the LORD will guide you continually, and satisfy your desire with good things** (Isaiah 58:6–11, emphasis added).

When I was seeking a wife, I frequently thought about Isaiah 58 and Genesis 24. With expectant hope (and a few anxieties), I trusted that God would bring the right woman into my life. At the time, I was engaged in a challenging youth ministry. My expectation was that God would take care of my needs if I busied myself in shepherding the teens under my care.

I met my wife, Karen, right in the middle of the church building where I conducted my youth ministry. God providentially brought Karen all the way from New York to a Florida youth ministry so we could meet and get married. It took me very little time to realize that God exceeded all my hopes, expectations, and prayers in bringing Karen into my life.

Someone has said that it's difficult to steer a docked boat. A boat needs to be moving before the rudder can guide its course. In the same way, you'll most likely find God's guidance as you serve wholeheartedly at the tasks He's called you to do.

Don't just stay at home hoping for a wife to drop down the chimney. Serve at conferences, in your church, in a catechism class, in a youth group, in a Boy Scout troop, in a pro-life group, or in a community group. Give primacy to serving the needs of others. Pray—especially in the presence of the Blessed Sacrament.

Ask others to pray.[46] Ask for the intercession of the saints and for the guidance of the angels. Finally, trust that God will answer your prayers and give you a good wife.

"The LORD is near to all who call upon Him, to all who call upon Him in truth. He fulfills the desire of all who fear Him" (Psalm 145:18–19).

CHAPTER SEVENTEEN

Q

Questions to Ask Before Saying, "I Do"

Pick up a book with a title such as *How to Interview Anyone* or *The Secrets to Dynamic Conversation*, and you'll find that good questions are the keys to unlocking the mind and heart of even the most guarded person. Asking good questions of a prospective wife is an excellent way to get to know her, as well as her plans and expectations for married life.

Before asking the deep, probing questions, it's generally best to start with comfortable openers such as "What's your favorite flavor of ice cream?" or "What's your favorite type of music?" In time, you'll be ready to move on to deeper topics. More sensitive topics, such as health status, previous marriages, bankruptcies, psychological treatments, and abusive family situations might best be asked by a marriage counselor or pastor.

Here's a sample list of questions you can use in conversation. You'll see some similar questions on the FOCCUS, PRE-PARE, and RELATE instruments. You can easily think up at least a few dozen more questions to ask. Don't just day-dream and wonder about what a woman thinks. Ask her!

"What are your favorites?"

What are your favorite restaurants?

What is your favorite type of music?

What are your favorite things to do on a weekend?

What are your favorite books?

What are your favorite movies?

What are your favorite TV shows?

What are your favorite sports?

Family background

What are some of your best family memories from childhood?

How did your family celebrate the holidays?

Did your family move much during your childhood?

What kind of relationship do you have with your mother and father?

What is your parents' marriage like?

Which of your parents paid the monthly bills for your family?

Which of your parents led family prayer time, if you had one?

How were major decisions made by your parents?

How was affection expressed in your family?

How was anger expressed in your family?

Is there any history of alcoholism in your immediate or extended family?

What is your relationship with your siblings like?

What did your family do on vacations?

Personal traits

Are you a "go-getter," a "laid-back" person, or somewhere in between?

Are you a "neatnik," a happy but messy person, or in between?

Would you describe yourself as an "outgoing," a "moderately outgoing," or a "private" person?

Do you prefer staying in or going out?

What do you do when under a lot of stress?

What annoys you?

How would you describe your temper?

What are your best and worst habits?

Is there anything important about you that you haven't told me yet?

Attitudes about children

Have you spent any time around young children over the past several years?

Do you like being around children?

Do you think daycare is a good idea for young children?

What do you think is the ideal number of children in a family?

What type of education would you want for your children (public, private, parochial, homeschool)?

Would you want your children to attend college? Any particular colleges?

Child rearing and discipline

How did your parents discipline you as a child?

What type of child discipline do you believe in?

Have you read any books or listened to any tapes on child discipline?

Who do you think should be primarily responsible for a child's discipline: the father or the mother?

Work and family finances

What jobs have you held?

Do you like your work?

What are your thoughts on a mother working outside the home?

Are you interested in being a career woman? If yes, what type of career?

What are your thoughts on home-based businesses?

If you received a $100,000 inheritance, what would you do with it?

What types of things are you willing to go into debt for?

What do you think are acceptable levels of family debt?

What level of ambition towards a career do you think a husband should have?

Do you give to religious and other charitable concerns?

Are you more of a saver or a spender?

The future and family life

Do you have desires or plans for any further career, college, or graduate education?

What would you like to be doing ten years from now?

What are your life goals?

Where would you expect to celebrate Thanksgiving and Christmas (and other holidays) after you're married?

Practicing the Faith

Do you have any type of daily prayer or devotions, such as reading the Bible?

Would you want your family to pray together?

Which religious leaders do you look up to?

Do you take any exceptions to the moral teaching of the Church?

CHAPTER EIGHTEEN

R

Romeo Online

New technology can spark courtship correspondence. Expanding railroads and improved roads in the nineteenth century provided speedier mail service. Courtship correspondence flourished as a result of these technological improvements. The golden age of American courtship correspondence was from about 1800 to 1880.

During this golden age, couples wrote to each other frequently—sometimes after only a few hours apart. Courtship correspondence was an invaluable means of both establishing and deepening relationships. Perhaps you would be surprised that men did the lion's share of letter writing during this period.

Correspondence was a valuable part of courtship for two particular reasons. First, writing each other allowed couples to get better acquainted without endangering their relationship with excessive physical intimacy—a difficult balancing act in every generation. Second, men weren't ashamed to express themselves in warm, romantic, and heartfelt ways. Here's just one line from a letter in 1808 that an eligible woman in any generation would enjoy receiving: "Excepting my obligation to God, my heart, my affections, my undivided and unreserved love are yours."[47]

Ecclesiastes says, "What has been is what will be, and what has been done is what will be done; and there is nothing new under the sun" (1:9). With the technological advances of the Internet and e-mail, romances developed through online correspondence are flourishing. It seems as though history is indeed repeating itself.

Given this situation, two characteristics from the golden age of courtship correspondence should be brought forward to the twenty-first century. First, letters of that period were phrased with great diligence. Correspondence was polished before being written with the finest penmanship. The slang and broken grammar used with AOL's Instant Messenger is fine for fun and informal online chatter, but we also need to use e-mail to correspond through deeper and more thoughtful letters.

Expressing affections online

The second characteristic needing resurrection from the golden age of correspondence is that men of that time were romantically expressive in their letters. In fact, many women during this period felt that correspondence brought out more of a man's inner soul than face-to-face conversations. I think they were correct. Courtship correspondence seemed to bring out the best in men, especially helping them overcome their perpetual difficulty in expressing themselves verbally.

It's tough for most men, even tough guys, to communicate what they feel for their wives. A good example is Mike Alstott, the 248-pound fullback with the Tampa Bay Bucs. The unstoppable "A-Train," as Alstott is affectionately known, just lowers his upper body and plows forward, leaving players flattened on the field.

Yet there is another side to the "A-Train." Mike is known as a family man who adores his wife and children. But Mike admits that he gets verbal paralysis when it comes to expressing his emotions to his wife, Nicole.

The three little words

Today, many men literally can't bring themselves to write three little words, "I love you," on a Valentine's Day card. Millions of other men find it impossible to look their wives in the eye and say, "I love you." For those of you who don't believe this, next Valentine's Day carefully read the dozens of cards saying something like this: "For all the times I wanted to say I love you but didn't. . . . I am giving you this card."

Nice touch in a card, but not sufficient verbal expression for the vast majority of wives. The guy whose communication skills are stretched by saying, "Whassup!" on Instant Messenger isn't the guy who will satisfy his wife's heart in marriage.

"Spring training" for developing communication skills

The courting period is the "spring training" season for developing your communication skills. Your verbal communication in marriage will usually not rise above the level it reaches during courtship, unless intervention and training take place (such as what we do at our St. Joseph's Covenant Keepers conferences). So muster the courage to write love letters online during your courtship. Be an online Romeo. That special woman in your life loves to hear, "You've got mail!"

Questions and answers—an easy way to get to know each other

In your online courtship correspondence, you can use e-mail to send questions such as the list of suggestions in the previous chapter for getting better acquainted. Just don't scan and send all the questions at one time! That could be a bit overwhelming, and it would resemble an interrogation more than communication. Just allow one question and answer to lead naturally to another related, and perhaps deeper, question.

Online precautions

While I'm enthusiastic about online romance, I urge you to take precautions when you meet someone online. Avoid about ninety-five percent of online chat rooms. You should always be cautious about giving out any personal information online. If you take this route, I suggest that you meet someone in a monitored Christian site.

Even these Christian sites are not fail-safe. I've read reports of people hiding personal information, making misleading statements, and even outright lying on some Christian singles sites. A Christian site requiring registration will minimize these deceptions. Nevertheless, you still need to practice discernment at any singles site. For a list of some good Christian Web sites, visit our Web site, www.familylifecenter.net, and click on "Courtship."

Honoring parents while practicing courtship in cyberspace

A timeless courtship principle is to honor both your parents. For a young man especially, this includes honoring a woman's father as the guardian and loving leader of her family. So how do you practice family-centered courtship practices in cyberspace?

Here's how the principle of involving parents might work in cyberspace. Suppose you want to court, or just get to know more seriously, a woman who's a member of an online singles community you've joined. As a gentlemen, you first ask for her permission to correspond. You also ask for her father's phone number. Simply explain to her that you want to request her father's permission to develop a relationship with her and that you want to express your intentions.

Does all this sound radical? You bet. Yet remember that the Fourth Commandment contains a divine promise to bless the lives of those who obey the commandment to honor parents. Your blessing may come in the way of strong support from her father.

Here's an amazing message I received from a Catholic father deeply moved by a young man wanting to court his daughter:

> Two months ago my 25-year-old daughter began a courtship with a gentleman. This man, in conversation with my daughter one evening, asked to speak with me. After a hello and some small talk, he asked if my wife and I would be available some evening that week to sit down and talk.

The week was busy for us, but we got together on Saturday and had one of the most unforgettable conversations I've ever had. He asked for permission to court our daughter and then asked if we could pray together for their relationship. Wow! It nearly blew me away. It was something I had only hoped would happen.

Often fathers and the young men interested in their daughters have an adversarial relationship. The earlier in your relationship you make the "permission from her father" call, the higher the probability that her father will be your advocate, rather than an adversary.

Bottom line? Use dear old Dad along with new technology to make electronic courtship a success.

CHAPTER NINETEEN

S

Scarcity of Good Women . . . and What You Can Do About It

The pastor introducing our first courtship conference mentioned that many young men come to him lamenting their difficulties in meeting a good Christian woman. He also said that many young women similarly lament that they can't find a good Christian man. His conclusion was, "Don't give up! They're out there."

Many single Christian women feel there's a greater scarcity of eligible Christian men. I believe that this feeling has a factual basis, due to the lower participation of males in church life. Yet many men are having difficulty meeting and marrying a good Christian woman. The singles scene is continually expanding, but finding a good Christian spouse in the midst of it all can be trying.

Things to do despite the scarcity of good women

What should a Christian man eager to find a suitable Christian mate do? Here are seven steps that will help you overcome the scarcity problem:

1. Avoid pity parties.

The first thing is to avoid pity parties with friends. These feed discouragement and bitterness. Most of all, avoid the "woe is me I'll never find a wife" attitude. Such despairing activities will breed faithlessness and hopelessness in your heart. Athletes, businessmen, and performers realize that they need a positive mental attitude to succeed. If you have a cheerful, optimistic outlook, you'll be much more attractive to a prospective spouse.

2. Get beyond the distance problem.

While I know that there are many good eligible Christian women, I can't guarantee that one lives on your block. Be open to the idea that God might have a prospective wife for you who lives far away.

I recently read the story of a woman from Wyoming on a Christian singles Web site who restricted the men wishing to correspond with her to those living in her region of the country. One particularly persistent man living in an entirely different part of the country kept writing her. She asked why he kept writing her since he lived so far away.

He answered that if he won a cash prize on a millionaire show, he would gladly cross the country to claim his prize. He felt that a good wife would be more valuable than a million-dollar prize. Humbly taken aback, she changed her mind and invited this man to keep writing her. They are now married.

Why not be willing to travel to find a good wife? I have friends who make road trips across three states to see their favorite team play. I have other friends who travel across half a continent into the wilderness to get to a favorite fish-ing spot. If guys can travel for fish and football, certainly they can travel for meeting a good wife.

Don't let distance be an obstacle in courting. Yes, the distance between families can make practicing courtship principles a little more difficult, but the principles can be successfully adapted to various circumstances.

3. Keep your eyes open for women you already know.

The psalmist prayed, "Open my eyes, that I may behold wondrous things out of Thy law"(Psalm 119:18). Many of you have had the experience of reading a familiar passage of Scripture for years when one day a verse just leaps off the page at you with sudden relevance.

The same type of thing might happen with a woman you've known for years without having any romantic notions about her. Since it wasn't yet time for you to court, God might have put a veil over the eyes of your heart. But then, when it's the proper time to start courting, you might suddenly discover in a new way this woman you've known for so long.

Heather worked as the church secretary and Thom worked on the construction of the church school, so they saw each other daily. Before Heather and Thom developed an interest in each other, friends thought that they might be suited for each other. Yet it took a year and a half for both Heather and Thom to realize that they should start a relationship to see whether they were meant for each other.

You never know which one God might bring you from far away or from close at hand.

4. Accept assistance from good matchmakers.

Families interested in adopting a child have found that letting their friends know of their serious desire to adopt can shorten the waiting period from years to months. In a similar way, your friends can be of tremendous assistance in finding you a prospective spouse, just as Heather and Thom's co-workers did in the story above. Wise friends may spot good possibilities before you do. So you shouldn't be embarrassed to let your close friends know that you're ready to find a good wife.

Watching the matchmaker in the movie *Fiddler on the Roof* may frighten you into never letting someone play that role for you. Yet you should be open to suggestions from family members and close friends with good judgment.

I remember reading a story of a church-going couple who noticed a handsome young man who made a regular practice of attending a Holy Hour.[48] This couple happened to be friends with an attractive young woman who was having difficulty meeting a young man who took his faith as seriously as she did. The couple encouraged their meeting. This young man and woman are now married.

One marriage and relationship expert stated the dramatic finding that sixty-three percent of married couples were first introduced to each other by friends or family.[49] Don't close your ears to the advice of reliable friends and family members. There isn't a successful businessman alive who doesn't appreciate the value of networking. Why not let friends and family networking work for you?

5. Use the Internet.

I think the Internet will quickly replace singles bars and church singles groups as a prime meeting place for people looking for a mate. Singles bars have their obvious limitations. Most church singles groups also have limitations in that they try to reach too wide a spectrum of people with very diverse interests and needs. You might find the average church singles group to include never-married twenty-year-olds grouped together with twice-married divorcees and in some cases with widows and widowers.

The Internet can quickly group you with people of similar age, background, and beliefs. The Internet also has an uncanny ability to bring people together with similar interests. Cyberspace is thus one of the most effective places to meet other Christian singles, especially if you live in a community with few women your age who share your faith.

Remember that your discernment must not be put on hold just because you use a Christian singles site. Some Christian singles sites are far better than others. Spend your time on the sites that have developed a solid reputation.

Is it an act of desperation to join a Christian singles site? Even though many feel this way, it really isn't. An act of desperation is looking for a wife in a singles bar, or even worse, lowering your standards for a wife because you can't meet someone who shares your faith. Using the Internet in the manner we've described is a wise way to keep your standards high and maximize your chances of meeting someone with similar beliefs, life goals, and interests.

6. Go where the like-minded women are.

If you want to catch a fish, you go where you think the most fish are. If you want to make a sales contact, you attend meetings with the greatest likelihood of finding potential clients. If you want to find a good wife, it makes sense to go to those locations and events where you know a group of good women is likely to be gathered.

One good place is a regional religious conference, especially those organized for singles committed to courtship.[50] Conferences such as these tend to draw committed believers from an entire geographic area. Another excellent location for finding a good wife is at a Christian college.

7. Seize your moments of opportunity.

Your chances of finding a good wife are greater if you're open to meeting someone while you're in your twenties than if you're in your thirties or forties. The reason is quite simple: There's a larger pool of eligible women in the younger years.

Does this mean that your prospects for finding a good wife evaporate after age thirty? No, not at all. In fact, some young men might feel a call to serve God for several years as a single person before seeking a partner in marriage. Just remember that being a godly husband and father is a challenging way for a dedicated Christian man to serve God.

You do need to consider carefully whether you're putting excessive career pursuits ahead of seeking a wife. It is necessary to undertake reasonable breadwinner preparations and training before marriage, but you don't need to get rich before you get married. Don't put family life on hold just to achieve ambitious career goals.

If you wanted to play for the NFL, you wouldn't wait until your 30s to try out for a team. Likewise, if marriage is one of your life priorities, you shouldn't allow a career to crowd out your best years for finding a wife.

CHAPTER TWENTY

T

"To Have and To Hold . . ."

To have and to hold, for better, for worse, for richer, for poorer, in sickness and in health, from this day forward, until death do us part."

You and your future wife will need the assurance that you will love and treasure each other throughout life. A marriage built upon an unconditional commitment of lifelong fidelity will give the two of you the confidence to give yourselves unreservedly to each other. Lasting marital love requires the spousal commitment to be total, exclusive, and faithful.[51]

Nevertheless, our culture has eroded almost all the traditional supports for lifelong marriage. It used to be that only Hollywood movie stars dissolved their marriages at whim. Now people from every segment of our entire society act this way, including Christians.

It used to be that when a middle-aged husband ran off with his 20-something bleached-blonde secretary, we called him what he was: a despicable, dirty, rotten scoundrel. Today, we just shrug it off with the lame excuse that he's suffering from a midlife crisis. In many states it's almost as easy to get a divorce as it is to get a driver's license. The astounding rates of divorce have eroded confidence in marriage, especially among young men and women. In response to this lowered trust in marriage, many couples are approaching it with timidity instead of certainty.

Contemporary couples often start out in marriage with a "let's try it and see if it works out" attitude. But these couples aren't ready for marriage. Nor are couples ready to wed who feel that they need a prenuptial agreement to serve as a legal parachute for their marriage.

Christian couples aren't prepared for marriage if they hold the poisonous attitude that says, "If our marriage doesn't work out, we can get a 'Christian divorce.'" Despite what you might read or hear on the airwaves, there's no such thing as a divorce from a valid Christian marriage, as Jesus made unmistakably clear in Mark 10:2–12.[52]

The *Catechism*, describing the fidelity required for marriage, says this:

> Love seeks to be definitive; it cannot be an arrangement "until further notice." The "intimate union of marriage, as a mutual giving of two persons, and the good of the children, demand total fidelity from the spouses and require an unbreakable union between them." The deepest reason is found in the fidelity of God to His covenant, in that of Christ to His Church.
>
> It can seem difficult, even impossible, to bind oneself for life to another human being. This makes it all the more important to proclaim

the Good News that God loves us with a definitive and irrevocable love, that married couples share in this love, that it supports and sustains them, and that by their own faithfulness they can be witnesses to God's faithful love.[53]

The two "C" words: commitment and covenant

Many men and women today are scared of the word *commitment*. In fact, some men go into complete panic when they hear the "C" word. Yet one-hundred percent commitment is required for a successful marriage. If you or a prospective spouse are not capable of making a total and complete commitment to each other, then you need to postpone marriage plans until you're ready to do so.

Successful marriages aren't built upon 50/50 commitments. That's only for civil contracts. Marriage covenants are made when spouses unreservedly give one hundred percent of themselves to each other.

In marriage, nothing is held in reserve. Nothing is excluded in the mutual giving of spouses to each other. This total and mutual self-giving is what joins the husband and wife, previously two separate individuals living two separate lives, into a new and mysterious oneness. The Bible says that they are no longer two, but one (see Genesis 2:24). There's nothing in all of human life quite like the mystery of marital oneness.

Because of its essential nature, the marriage covenant excludes everyone except one spouse. So long as the two of you are still alive, no one is allowed to take your place for any reason. Since marriage is a living icon of the faithful bond that Christ has for His Church, marital infidelity or divorce can never be considered as an option for a valid Christian marriage. That's why Christian couples are required to pledge solemn vows in the presence of God to have lifelong fidelity toward each other.

I compare the confidence needed in marriage to the confidence a sailor needs in the ship's anchor. Whenever I'm sleeping on a boat at anchor, I don't permit myself to get lost in a good night's sleep, even though I may be exhausted from a long day on the water. Throughout the night, I listen to the waves slapping against the side of the boat as an indication that the wind hasn't switched directions, making it easy for the anchor to lose its hold. Only when I have complete assurance of a secure mooring can I rest easily.

Similarly, marital love can't flourish in a climate of doubt. If you don't have assurance of total, exclusive, and faithful love, then you'll be plagued with nagging worries. Will she divorce me in ten years? Would she still love me if my health changed, or if I were disabled by a stroke or an automobile accident?

The pre-engagement period is the best time for close second and third evaluations. Even during the engagement period evaluations can be made. This book has probably encouraged more premarital consideration than most of the advice you've heard to date. Yet caution and hesitancy are appropriate *before* marriage. Once you're married, the time for second thoughts is over—forever. Married life is the time for reckless abandonment to unconditional love.

CHAPTER TWENTY-ONE

U

Ultimate Marriage Buster

A study commissioned by the Marriage Project at Rutgers University found that eighty percent of young people say their number-one priority is a lasting marriage. Surely every marriage should begin with soaring hopes and expectations for a lifetime of love. Your wedding day should be the day when your dreams come true. So why are so many marital dreams turning into the nightmare of divorce?

Reasons abound for the multitude of marital breakups occurring all around us. I've tried to identify many of the reasons in this book so you can avoid them. Nevertheless, one particular contributor to divorce stands out above all others. This ultimate marriage buster is *contraception*, embraced by ninety-seven percent of young married couples even though it threatens the core of their marital relationship.

Five hundred percent increase In the divorce rate

The divorce rate has increased five hundred percent since the ultimate marriage buster started gaining popular acceptance early in the twentieth century. The ultimate marriage buster was given a big boost by medical technology in the 1960s, and the divorce rate has doubled since then. In fact, the divorce rate for new marriages hovers at fifty percent. In stark contrast, those married couples wise enough to keep the marriage buster out of their bedrooms have a divorce rate under five percent.[54]

Divorce has become a national concern. Government leaders, social agencies, university researchers, church leaders, and marital counselors are diligently searching for ways to improve marital stability. Individual Americans are spending more than a hundred million dollars every year on books, tapes, seminars, and therapy in an attempt to discover the secret glue that will hold contemporary marriages together. Strangely absent in our national search for marital stability is a public recognition and identification of the practice of contraception as the ultimate buster of modern marriage.

Why does avoiding the ultimate marriage buster cause the probability of divorce to plummet from fifty percent to less than five percent? To answer this critical question, you must know something about the uniqueness of marital love between spouses.

Marital love involves the innermost being of husband and wife

If asked, millions of Americans probably couldn't answer the question, "What's the difference between two animals copulating and a husband and wife expressing love in the marital embrace?" Yet the difference is deeply significant. While animal copulation is something purely biological, marital love is much, much more. Listen carefully to what the *Catechism* says:

Sexuality, by means of which man and woman give themselves to one another through the acts which are proper and exclusive to spouses, is not something simply biological, but concerns the innermost being of the human person as such. It is realized in a truly human way only if it is an integral part of the love by which a man and woman commit themselves totally to one another until death.[55]

Total giving in marital love

Marital love is expressed in the total giving of oneself—body, mind, and heart—to one's spouse. This profound union goes beyond just the union of bodies. It's the complete union of persons joining the innermost cores of their being.

That's why the *Catechism* goes on to say that "conjugal love involves a totality, in which all the elements of the person enter—appeal of the body and instinct, power of feeling and affectivity, aspiration of the spirit and of will. It aims at a deeply personal unity, a unity that, beyond union in one flesh, leads to forming one heart and soul; it demands *indissolubility* and *faithfulness* in definitive mutual giving; and it is open to *fertility*."[56]

The Berlin Wall between spouses

Contraception erects a Berlin Wall between spouses, frustrating the intimate union of marriage. Contraception speaks in silent language, "I give you some of myself, maybe even most of myself, but not all of myself." This partial giving creates a corrosive selfishness at the core of your marital union.

In contrast, genuine marital love, expressed in a sacred language of the body, says, "I give you myself—all of myself—without reservation." What happens when marital love is expressed in this total, self-giving manner? The *Catechism* describes it this way: "The acts in marriage by which the intimate and chaste union of the spouses takes place are noble and honorable; the truly human performance of these acts fosters the self-giving they signify and enriches the spouses in joy and gratitude."[57]

Breaking commandments leads to broken marriages

By practicing contraception, couples not only shut out their love for each other; they also damage their relationship with God. Breaking God's commands in marriage results in a multitude of broken marriages.

Since the first marriage in the Garden of Eden, God has commanded two purposes for marriage: *love making* (the unitive: "the two shall become one flesh," Genesis 2:24) and *life giving* (the procreative: "be fruitful and multiply," Genesis 1:28). Just as it is with the damage from cohabitation, when we engage in practices at odds with our Creator's design, things break. When we sever the bond of *love making* from *life giving*, marriages break—by the millions.

The twofold purpose of marriage

The *Catechism* continues this original teaching on marriage:

> The spouses' union achieves the twofold end of marriage: the good of the spouses themselves and the transmission of life. These two meanings or values of marriage cannot be separated without altering the couple's spiri-

tual life and compromising the goods of marriage and the future of the family.

So the Church . . . teaches that "it is necessary that each and every marriage act must remain ordered *per se* to the procreation of human life. This particular doctrine, expounded on numerous occasions by the Magisterium, is based on the inseparable connection, established by God, which man on his own initiative may not break, between the unitive significance and the procreative significance which are both inherent to the marriage act."[58]

Christian morality thus forbids any sexual activity that separates the unitive and procreative purposes, including masturbation, homosexual acts, sterilization (vasectomies or tubal ligations), contraception, and acts consciously intended to interrupt coitus and thwart procreation.

An ecumenical morality—until recently

For nineteen out of the past twenty centuries, *all* Christian denominations forbade these practices as gravely sinful. Most modern readers are surprised to learn that *all* the major Protestant leaders such as Martin Luther, John Calvin, and John Wesley taught that contraception and unnatural acts to thwart procreation destroyed the souls of those engaging in such practices.[59]

Natural Family Planning

The sacredness of the marital union is not violated when couples enjoy their embrace during infertile times. So if there are serious reasons to limit or space births, couples can morally practice what is called Natural Family Planning (NFP).

When used for proper reasons, Natural Family Planning doesn't violate the twofold ends of marriage (*love making* and *life giving*).

The trustworthy teaching of the papal encyclical *Humanae Vitae [Of Human Life]* says: "If, then, there are serious motives to space out births . . . it is then licit to take into account the natural rhythms immanent in the generative functions, for the use of marriage in the infecund [infertile] periods only, and in this way to regulate birth without offending the moral principles which have been recalled earlier."[60]

A first-rate premarital training program should regard thorough training in Natural Family Planning as important as communication, compatibility, and family finances. Some premarital classes devote only a few minutes to Natural Family Planning; other classes completely ignore the topic. Both of these approaches are huge mistakes. Make certain that you have NFP training, even if you have to go outside your premarital classes to get it. NFP classes are taught throughout the country by competent couples.[61]

Assault against fatherhood

The contraception movement is a deceptive assault against fatherhood.[62] As a man, one of your highest privileges in married life is cooperating with God in bringing forth a new life. Nothing else you ever do will have such lasting importance.

By promising unlimited sexual pleasure without any of the responsibilities of fatherhood, the contraception movement deceives men into various forms of fatherhood castration. In Old Testament days a person's hand was cut off for grabbing a man's private parts during a fight (see Deuteronomy

25:11–12). A century ago, a man might have shot another person who threatened his procreative ability. Now millions of men voluntarily pay thousands of dollars for the mutilation of their ability to father children. Before ever taking such a drastic step yourself, read the advice from men who deeply regret having a vasectomy.[63]

Christians during the twentieth century were foolish enough to imagine that abandoning God's design for marital love would bring liberation and happiness. In your selection of a wife, be certain that you have a solemn agreement with your fiancée to keep the ultimate marriage buster completely out of your marriage. You don't want to repeat the last century's mistakes.

CHAPTER TWENTY-TWO

V

Vocation of Marriage

Most of us hear the word *vocation* and think of a career, a profession, an occupation, or a trade. The word comes from a Latin root meaning *to call*. The Catholic teaching on vocation is that God personally calls us to a particular path He has laid out for us to follow in life. This divine call involves far more than an occupational decision. It's a call from God to a particular state of life: the vocations of marriage, the priesthood, consecrated life in a religious order, single life, or the permanent diaconate.[64]

Focus on your vocation

The Catholic understanding of the vocation of marriage is particularly helpful in our culture, which tends to assume that your work defines who you are and that the level of your salary determines your personal worth. The Church teaches us, on the contrary, that while our jobs are important, they should never eclipse the importance of the vocation of marriage.

Our culture is ready to lead the married into an all-consuming spousal relationship with their careers. The resulting misplaced priorities invariably damage marriage and family life. When the regrets finally surface, it's often too late to make up for the lost time. If God is calling you to the vocation of marriage, then you must stay focused on your vocation.

Selecting a career to fit your vocation

Once you determine God's vocation for your life, you can select a career path that will enable you to fulfill your vocation. For instance, if God is calling you to be a husband and father, then it is wise to learn skills that would permit you to work in a career that would provide sufficiently for a growing family.

Many men select a career path without giving the slightest thought to how that career will influence their family life. For example, choosing a high-salary career that demands continual out-of-town travel is not a family-friendly choice. Also, think twice before taking a job with one of the many 24/7 businesses that will keep you on the corporate treadmill. As a father, you will face the twin challenges of finding income for adequate daily bread and a career allowing for enough daily family time. The most important ingredient in your success as a father is investing time in the lives of your children.[65] Don't wait until you become a dad to discover that, for children, love is a four-letter word spelled T-I-M-E.

What is the secret for finding enough family time in our hectic world with misplaced priorities? It is making your vocation as husband and father your top priority, and then choosing a career that is compatible with your vocation. It's possible for men to restore priorities later in life, but you will save yourself enormous frustration by getting focused on your vocation and compatible career as early as possible—ideally, before selecting a college major.

The need for quiet time in an age of noise

In order to hear your personal call, you need to give God some quiet time. I'll suggest something really radical. I recommend that you unplug your stereo for at least an hour every day and enjoy some quiet time.

Novelist Michael O'Brien has accurately described our times as an "age of noise."[66] Everywhere we go, all day long and well into the night, our electronic gadgets give us nonstop noise. So each of us needs to make some quiet time for meditation each day.

Mornings are the best time to listen to the gentle nudging of the Holy Spirit (see Psalm 119:147; Wisdom 16:28; Sirach 32:14, 39:5). With a listening heart read Scripture, pray, and just sit in silence. A quiet morning or evening walk is also a good way to maintain an open ear. Before making a major decision, I find a quiet hour in the church in the presence of the Blessed Sacrament to be indispensable for determining God's direction for me.

Whatever vocation God calls you to, it will be the path on which you'll find deep joy and satisfaction of heart. Make your vocation a life priority. If He's calling you to marriage, then joyfully follow Him on the path to holiness in married life. This call is twofold: first to marriage, and second to a specific person. Pray that God's will can be revealed so that you'll recognize the person He intends for you.

CHAPTER TWENTY-THREE

Wine—a Blessing and a Marriage Buster

One of my most enjoyable times after a long workweek is "date night" with my wife at one of our favorite restaurants, slowly sipping wine together. It's hard to imagine life getting better than this pleasant and relaxing way to share married life. Surely God is good in giving "wine to gladden the heart of man" (Psalm 104:15).

Nevertheless, my wife and I are willing to suspend our enjoyment of wine whenever we realize that those joining us for dinner abstain because they have an alcoholic family background or because they have personal struggles with alcoholism. Christian charity requires that we abstain if our actions could become a cause of stumbling. St. Paul says, "It is right not to eat meat or drink wine or do anything that makes your brother stumble. We who are strong ought to bear with the failings of the weak, and not to please ourselves" (Romans 14:21, 15:1).

For twenty-five years in family ministry, I've seen alcoholism's pernicious ability to mangle marriages and fracture families. Over and again, I've observed that it's a small step from merrymaking with wine to marital melancholy due to alcoholism. So if I thought either of us had crossed the threshold into the early stages of alcoholism, I'd abstain permanently. My marriage means infinitely more to me than a half carafe of wine.

Warnings about alcohol abuse

The Bible says that wine is a blessing from God. It was used in the Old Testament for sacrifices and rejoicing on feast days. Jesus performed His first miracle by turning water into wine at the wedding at Cana. St. Paul even said that wine mixed with water has medicinal value (1 Timothy 5:23).

Yet in contrast to all these positive biblical statements about alcohol, we also read a host of warnings about the dangers associated with too much of a good thing. Here's a sampling of the many biblical warnings and exhortations about drunkenness:

> "Let us conduct ourselves becomingly as in the day, not in reveling and drunkenness" (Romans 13:13).

> "Now the works of the flesh are plain . . . envy, drunkenness, carousing, and the like. I warn you, as I warned you before, that those who do such things shall not inherit the kingdom of God" (Galatians 5:19–21).

> "And do not get drunk with wine, for that is debauchery; but be filled with the Spirit" (Ephesians 5:18).

> "Let the time that is past suffice for doing what the Gentiles like to do, living in licentiousness,

passions, drunkenness, revels, carousing, and lawless idolatry"(1 Peter 4:3).

"Woe to those who are heroes at drinking wine, and valiant men in mixing strong drink" (Isaiah 5:22).

"Wine is a mocker, strong drink a brawler; and whoever is led astray by it is not wise" (Proverbs 20:1).

"Who has woe? Who has sorrow? Who has strife? Who has complaining? Who has wounds without cause? Who has redness of eyes? Those who tarry long over wine, those who go to try mixed wine. Do not look at wine when it is red, when it sparkles in the cup and goes down smoothly. At the last it bites like a serpent, and stings like an adder. Your eyes will see strange things, and your mind utter perverse things" (Proverbs 23:29–33).

Turning men into beasts and barbarians

Too much wine and whiskey can turn gentlemen into beasts and barbarians, bringing out the very worst in them. I thought that I'd seen a lot of drunken fighting in high school and on a major university campus. But that was nothing compared to what I saw sailors do when I was stationed in Guantanamo Bay, Cuba.

Being on an island military base surrounded by Communist troops, we didn't have much to do at night except drink. Kegs of cheap beer and hard liquor were consumed for hours on weeknights and on weekends at servicemen's clubs. Practically every night on the way back to their ships and barracks the Marines and Navy servicemen would provoke brutal fights with one another. Drunkenness made comrades nearly dismember each other.

Unfortunately for families, such drunken aggression is not limited to military bases. Too much alcohol can cause men to say and to do things to their families that they'll later deeply regret. Ask any law enforcement officer about the main ingredient in the endless cases of domestic abuse, and he'll tell you that booze leads to bruises. The first recorded instances of incest in the Bible followed drunkenness (see Genesis 19:30–36). Alcohol destroys millions of marriages every year, while leaving a legacy of scarred hearts in the children of alcoholics.

In addition, thousands of unmarried men and women have succumbed to sexual temptation because they had too much to drink while on a date. You'd be wise to keep all your senses about you while courting.

A letter that can prevent a lifetime of misery

The wisest commentary I've ever read on alcoholism is a two-page letter from Dr. Anderson Spickard, professor of medicine at the Vanderbilt Medical Center and director of the Vanderbilt Center for the Treatment of Alcoholism. Through his research and experience, Dr. Spickard has determined that *the majority of our nation's ten million alcoholics come from families with an inherited tendency.*[67]

One special study highlighting the genetic predisposition for alcoholism focused on men who had alcoholic fathers but were adopted at birth by other families. Even without the environmental influence of being raised by their alcoholic fathers, these men were found to be nine times as likely to develop an addiction as children of non-alcoholic fathers.[68]

Dr. Spickard warns that alcoholism travels down family lines to such a degree that sixty percent to eighty percent of alcoholics have parents, grandparents, siblings, aunts or uncles who are also alcoholics.

Dr. Spickard writes his two-page letter to the children and grandchildren of the alcoholics he treats. He warns them of the genetic disposition for alcoholism and suggests total abstinence as the wisest preventative. You too should heed his warning: There's great wisdom in abstaining if either you or your future spouse have a family history of alcoholism.

Many men fall for the charms of an outgoing gal who's the life of every party. Only too late do they realize they've married an alcoholic who deprives their marriage of happiness and warps their home into a living hell. If you're courting a woman addicted to drinking, then I'd suggest you attend a couple of Alcoholics Anonymous meetings to sober up your marital decision-making process.

Wine in moderation is a blessing from God to gladden hearts. Yet alcohol taken to excess is heartbreaking. *Temperance* is not a dirty word. It's the virtue that, according to the *Catechism*, "moderates the attraction of pleasures and provides balance in the use of created goods. It ensures the will's mastery over instincts and keeps desires within the limits of what is honorable."[69] Make sure that the woman you marry is a temperate woman.

CHAPTER TWENTY-FOUR

X-Ray Her Words and Her Heart

I'm sure you've received the spam e-mails promising "to find out anything about anyone" using Internet background searches. Here's a better way to find out what's really inside someone: Listen attentively, if you want to know what's in a woman's heart. Wisdom from the book of Sirach says, "If you love to listen you will gain knowledge, and if you incline your ear you will become wise" (6:33).

Active listening

In premarital and marital counseling, I've found that careful listening is the most important skill I have to offer a couple. Truly attentive listening is work and requires concentration, but it always rewards the listener with knowledge of the other person. Speech is the window into the heart. Jesus said, "The tree is known by its fruit ... For out of the abundance of the heart the mouth speaks. The good man [and woman] out of his good treasure brings forth good, and the evil man out of his evil treasure brings forth evil" (Matthew 12:33–35).

Good women use kind speech

The type of woman you're interested in is hesitant to gossip; speaks kindly of others, even those she disagrees with; uses her tongue with kindness to build others up; and always speaks respectfully to her parents and family members.

The consequences of marrying a woman with an unruly tongue

The type of woman you want to avoid is quick to give others a tongue-lashing, is frequently critical of others, is argumentative, uses biting sarcasm, or is always complaining. Be warned that if you marry a woman sharply critical of others, then you will most certainly find her harshly critical of you. If you hear her verbally tear down others, then her tongue will be slashing at her husband. If her tongue shoots forth biting sarcasm, then be assured that her sarcastic arrows will be directed at you in marriage. Proverbs warns that "a wife's quarreling is a continual dripping of rain" and that "it is better to live in a corner of the housetop than in a house shared with a contentious woman" (19:13; 21:9).

In contrast, a good wife's tongue refreshes the spirit of her husband. Proverbs says, "A gentle tongue is a tree of life" (15:4). So X-Ray the heart of any woman you become interested in by carefully listening to her. What you hear is a good predictor of what will come out of her mouth in marriage.

CHAPTER TWENTY-FIVE

Y

Your Move! What Are You Waiting For?

The previously well known path through courtship to marriage has been overgrown with thorns. Instead of clearly defined cultural roles for courting men and women, men today are left to figure out by themselves what to do. For many men, this is like being tossed into a championship game as a quarterback without having a playbook. It would not be a surprise in such a situation if the referee blew his whistle for too much time in the huddle.

Too much time in the huddle

Many young Christian men are spending too much time in the huddle, frozen in uncertainty regarding their courting roles. It is understandable that you might tend to do nothing if you are uncertain of what to do. Yet the adventure of selecting a lifelong marriage partner doesn't reward those who play it ultrasafe from the sidelines, or in an extended huddle.

There certainly is a time for reading and learning about the mate selection process, but there is also a time to move into action. For many of you reading this book, it is past time for action.

Here's the play–now execute!

If you've reached the stage in life when you are ready to court, then it's time to execute the time-honored courtship play. Here it is:

The man woos, the woman is wooed. The man initiates the courtship and the woman responds. This is the play that will put you into action.

Don't pay attention to the confusing messages coming from the stands (our post-Christian culture). Men are supposed to take the initiative. If you are at the stage of life to court, then what are you waiting for? It's time to step out and start actively seeking a wife.

Don't be afraid of marriage

Risk is unavoidable if you want to achieve anything great. Entrusting your love to another person in the sacrament of marriage involves risk. But as Pope John Paul II has repeated throughout his pontificate, "Be not afraid!"

You should enjoy the abiding certainty that God is with you in the entire mate selection process. Don't be afraid of courtship and marriage. Do your part in the responsible choosing of a wife, but also be aware that in every step of the process you and your future wife are being upheld by God's hand.

St. Peter is sometimes overly criticized for his impetuous nature. When the disciples saw Jesus walking on the water, they were all terrified and cried out in fear. Yet only St. Peter had the faith to leave the security of the boat and walk to Jesus on the water. Fear and hesitancy kept all the others in the boat. Sure, St. Peter had his moment of doubt while walking on the water, but he cried out for the Savior's help. And according to St. Matthew, "Jesus immediately reached out his hand and caught him" (14:31).

If God has called you to marriage, don't let fear keep you from venturing on the path leading through courtship to marriage. The Bible says, "Do not deprive yourself of a wise and good wife, for her charm is worth more than gold" (Sirach 7:19). Marriage is one of life's greatest blessings, and it's worth the venture.

Prudence vs. prolonged delays

Throughout this book, I have advocated caution and deliberative decision making in choosing a spouse. Yet there is a difference between prudence and prolonged delays of courtship and postponement of marriage. Don't let commitment phobia and avoidance of risk rob you of one of life's greatest blessings.

Once you and your prospective mate have followed the steps recommended in this book and have a firm realization that you are meant for each other, do not let fear paralyze you from taking the final step in committing to marriage. At this point, you should be willing to propose, and the woman you are courting should be ready to give you a response.

Courting men should remember the encouraging words St. Raphael the archangel spoke to timid Tobias: "Do not be afraid, for she was destined for you from eternity . ... When Tobias heard these things, he fell in love with her and yearned deeply for her" (Tobit 6:17). If God has called you to the vocation of marriage, then His plan for you includes the blessings of a wife. Yet the fulfillment of this plan requires steps of faith on your part.

I'll conclude this chapter by switching to a stock car racing analogy. There is a time for prudent preparations in the pits. Then there is the scheduled time to move cars onto the track. Finally, the announcement is heard, "Gentlemen, start your engines." It's then time to put it into gear and get moving. The courting initiative belongs to you. Go for it.

CHAPTER TWENTY-SIX

Z

Zero in on What I'm Saying

I want your marriage to be a foretaste of heaven on earth. I want you to enjoy the blessings of a long, happy marriage. As I said in the introduction, by following and by doing *all* the ABC's, you should experience a seventy-five percent reduction in the probability of suffering a divorce. You should have great expectations for a happy, lifelong marriage.

The wise man and the foolish man

Yet listen very carefully. Just reading the ABC's, mentally agreeing with them, and having good intentions to practice them will have zero beneficial effect—unless your intentions are translated into action. Want a sneak preview of your future marriage and family life? You can learn your future by determining which type of man you are in Jesus' story of the wise and foolish men:

> Every one then who **hears** these words of mine **and does them** will be like a wise man who built his house upon the rock; and the rain fell, and the floods came, and the winds blew and

beat upon that house, but it did not fall, because it had been founded on the rock.

And every one who **hears** these words of mine and **does not do them** will be like a foolish man who built his house upon the sand; and the rain fell, and the floods came, and the winds blew and beat against that house, and it fell; and great was the fall of it.

MATTHEW 7:24–27

If you want a successful, lifelong Christian marriage, then you must do what God teaches about courtship, marriage, and sexual morality. One of the biggest pitfalls for Christians is to imagine that just attending a conference, reading a book, or hearing a sermon will positively impact their life.

Finding your way with a courtship map

You can take two steps to ensure that you become a "hearer and doer" and not just an inactive hearer. The first step is a written plan. This should come as no surprise if you are in the business world. You'll never get a business loan, or corporate funding for your division, without a written plan.

Your chances of becoming a successful "hearer and doer" at least triple with a *written* personal plan for your courtship. Most men are driven by appearances, passions, and emotional feelings while making the greatest decision of their life. A written plan functions as a map keeping you from getting lost in superficialities. Appendix I has tips and a sample list of items to include in writing your personal plan.

Keeping on course with a courtship GPS

If you are like most men, you also need to take a second step to stay on your courtship course. You need someone who can hold you accountable to your written plan for courtship. How many athletes have all the discipline necessary to make it to the playoffs without a coach? How many win an Olympic gold medal without a trainer? How many corporations make it into the Fortune 500 without managers and boards of directors to ensure accountability?

Without an accountability partner, my guess is that you have less than a 50/50 chance of sticking with all your courtship intentions. But you'll dramatically increase your chances of staying on course if you have a mature, clear-headed, male Christian friend to keep you on track with your courtship plan.

If a written personal plan is like a map through courtship to a successful marriage, then an accountability friend is like having a GPS. With both you won't get lost.

Don't learn about marriage the hard way

Many of us have to learn life's lessons the hard way before we become open to listening to wisdom. If you fit into this category, be warned: There's a huge difference between life lessons about marriage and life lessons about other experiences. Unlike many other mistakes in life, marriage mistakes have consequences that are internal and lifelong.

Marriage permanently bonds you—heart, soul, and body—to another person. If you make a big mistake in selecting a marriage partner, then the "oneness" of marriage cannot be completely undone. Even if you get a divorce and move a thousand miles from your estranged wife, a part of you will always be with her, and a part of her will always be with you. In the deepest part of your heart, the pain will be with you. If a divorce occurs with children, then this pain will travel on to the next generation.

For that reason, I urge you: After reading this book, put into action all that you've learned. The steps you take now while on the road toward marriage will have lasting effects for better or for worse.

The new wave of Christian marriages

My hope for your marriage is that it will become a part of a new wave of successful, lifelong Christian marriages in this new millennium. Christian marriages in the twentieth century failed at astonishing rates. You don't have to travel that road.

Furthermore, you have no need to be pessimistic about finding a good wife and having a successful marriage. Keep your standards high, carefully follow Christian principles, take action when it is called for, and have faith in the Good Shepherd leading you through this stage of life. He will lead you to the woman with whom you want to spend a lifetime.

May God grant you a godly, beautiful, and loving wife, along with many happy years of married life.

Appendix

Appendix I

Sample
Personal Courtship Commitments

I,_____ , hereby designate

_____ as my accountability

partner regarding the standards and commitments in my personal courtship plan listed below.

Brief description of accountability item (ABCs chapter number). *By referring to the ABCs chapter number, you are giving a fuller meaning and context to your brief commitment statement.*

- I will not date, court, or marry an immodest woman. (Ch. 1)

- I will take the time to really get to know the family of any woman that I am interested in. (Ch. 2)

- I will not overlook dysfunctions in family background. (Ch. 2)

- I will not engage in premarital sexual relations or cohabitation. We will not spend extensive time alone during our courtship and engagement. (Ch. 3)

- I will not allow excessive career pursuits to put aside marriage and family life. (Ch. 5)

- I will not marry someone desiring a permanent fulltime career, even when we have young children. (Ch. 7)

- I will only marry with the full blessing of her parents and mine. (Ch. 8)

- I will court and marry someone who fully shares my faith. (Ch. 9)

- To safeguard our relationship, we will postpone physical affection until we are married. (Ch. 10)

- My fiancée and I will take a premarital inventory before publicly announcing our engagement. (Ch. 12)

- I will marry someone who fully shares my commitment to the Church's teaching on sexuality. Once engaged, my fiancée and I will take classes on Natural Family Planning. (Ch. 21)

- I will not marry a binge drinker or a person who gets drunk. (Ch. 23)

I promise to notify my accountibility partner whenever I think that I might have an interest in courting someone. I give full permission to my accountability partner to use any lawful means to hold me accountable to my personal plan.

After serious reflection and with a firm reliance upon the grace of God, I commit myself to these standards when choosing a wife.

_____   _____
Signature   Date

_____   _____
Signature of accountability partner   Date

For a (PDF) printable form for developing your Personal Courtship Plan, go to www.familylifecenter.net and click on *Courtship*.

Increasing Your Chances of Sticking to Your Courtship Commitments

It's a known fact that most people don't follow through with their resolutions, despite good intentions.

It's best not to rush into writing your commitment list immediately after reading this book. Your commitments have a much higher probability of long-term success if they are preceded by a period of reflection and preparation. During this period it is important to focus on getting mentally and spiritually "geared" to really stick with your commitments and make them a part of your life.

Therefore, I recommend that you initially schedule (in writing) a date to write down your commitments after four weeks of reflection. In the meantime, you can review this book and make preparatory notes, as well as get good ideas from Neil Clark Warren's "must haves" and "can't stands" suggested lists.[70] During these four weeks, you might visit a divorce recovery group in your church, or have a long honest talk with a divorced person. Such a reality check will deepen your commitment process.

After your weeks of reflection and prayer, write out your commitments. Reflect upon your personal commitment list for at least two weeks before finalizing it. After that, announce your commitments to your accountability partner, enlist his support, and sign your commitments in his presence.

Research has shown that people who jump into commitments tend to jump out of them almost as quickly.[71] You can almost double the probability of sticking with your courtship commitments by progressively developing them in these suggested stages.[72]

Appendix II

(Note: *The Screwtape Letters,* a book by C.S. Lewis, unveils a series of secret correspondence between a senior demon, Screwtape, and his neophyte tempter and nephew Wormwood. Lewis uses a type of reverse theology to warn Christians against diabolical temptation strategies. The account below illustrates how Screwtape might advise utilizing the darker sides of the Internet to ensnare Christian men.)

Screwtape's Strategies to Destroy Family Life

My Dear Wormwood:

For your careful review, I have outlined below our strategies for destroying the Faith and family life. Destroy this secret message immediately after reading it. This classified material comes from the lowest regions.

In this new millennium, we must use technology to bring our master plan to completion by utilizing Internet pornography. Already we have spiritually neutralized millions of the Enemy's men with pornography. Over the next few years we can surely make millions more spiritual midgets, whom we can then manipulate at will.

It is so encouraging that Internet pornography has ensnared so many millions of young Christian men. These young fools think there is no harm in a few clicks to dirty Web sites. Little do they know that we can't wait to use their growing porn addiction to drive a wedge between them and their despicable brides.

You see, the delightful byproduct of pornography addiction is that it is so effective in creating turmoil in marriages. Of course, we have been attempting to destroy marriages as a vital part of our overall plan. A husband's pornography addiction has shown a unique ability to undermine trust and intimacy between spouses. The addiction creates turmoil, heartbreak, and bewilderment in the hearts of those detestable Christian wives. It's so amusing to watch marriages fall apart when husbands assume that their wives actually believe their deceptions and lies about not having a porn addiction.

With Internet pornography we can finally bring down the guardians of the Christian family. The fools still don't realize that the technological temptations are waging war against their very souls, bringing to completion a more-than-a-century-long campaign to destroy the Faith by destroying the family. Since it is working so exceedingly well, I suggest that we continue to use every technological innovation to pump pornography to Christian men. Just think of the wonderful new digital temptations we are sending out over broadband!

Remember, every man addicted to pornography is caught in the snares of what the Enemy calls grave sin. With pornography we have crippled their ability to spiritually protect themselves and their families. After they are ensnared in pornography, their families (their marriages and their children) are vulnerable to our attacks. Sure, these men still appear fine on the outside as they go to church, but we know that their hearts have been captured by pornography.

And since sons usually follow in their father's footsteps, the sins of the fathers will run down through the generations, and we can rest assured that the future generations will belong to us.

As far as Sundays in church go, there is only one thing to do. Just make sure things stay as they are—nice and quiet. The last thing we need are homilies about specific sins such as pornography. If a damaging homily is somehow preached, make sure you scramble any attempts to organize support groups to assist men unable to free themselves from our work. Just let the poor devils struggle alone—though of course we know that they are not alone in their pornography addiction, don't we?

Finally, we must keep up our guard against the Head of THAT family. Never forget how the Head of THAT family was used by the Enemy to ruin our dear servant Herod's plans to kill the so-called Holy One. There are centuries-old rumors from the upper regions that the Head of THAT family will be brought into service at a critical time in history. The last thing we want is a repeat of the first century.

It has taken immense effort, but we have managed thoroughly to confuse modern man (and much of the Church) about the meaning of true manhood and masculinity. We need impure men, especially husbands and fathers, to continue leading the culture towards our regions. We must therefore keep men from contact with the Head of THAT family, so that they don't have any effective models of manly purity and righteousness.

Yet we need to be realistic in our strategies. If we cannot keep men away from the Unmentionable One, then at least we can chip away at some of the truth to keep things manageable for us. Keep their beliefs abstract. Men look up to tangible role models. Just be sure they don't discover the Enemy's perfect model for husbands and fathers, or our plans will get derailed. We can never hope to lead fathers who are devoted to that so-called "Just Man" deeper into the depraved delights of pornography.

Yours diabolically,
Screwtape

Online Help for Those Struggling with Pornography:
http://dads.org/link.html
Web filtering software, Pure Mind Scripture software and memory
kits, and 12 Steps to Freedom from Pornography.

Endnotes

[1] See Maggie Gallagher and Linda J. Waite, *The Case for Marriage: Why Married People Are Happier, Healthier, and Better Off Financially* (New York: Doubleday, 2000).

[2] Adapted with permission from *Dynamic Preaching*, May 1989, Christian Communications Laboratory, P. O. Box 10965, Knoxville, TN 37939.

[3] David M. Buss *et al.*, "A Half Century of Mate Preferences: The Cultural Evolution of Values," *Journal of Marriage and Family*, 63 (May 2001), 491–503.

[4] See Judith S. Wallerstein, Julia M. Lewis, Sandra Blakeslee, *The Unexpected Legacy of Divorce: A 25-Year Landmark Study* (New York: Hyperion, 2000).

[5] The St. Michael's Institute (online go to www.saintmichael.net) is a national alliance of mental health professionals who integrate the genuine discoveries of psychology and psychiatry with the teaching of the Catholic Church. This organization is a good place to start in locating a counselor. The Institute for the Psychological Sciences in Arlington, Virginia, (phone: (703) 416-1441; Web site: www.cips-usa.org) is training a new generation of psychologists who also integrate their scientific and therapeutic careers with Christian faith. Talking with graduates from this Institute is another good starting place in your search for a good counselor.

Because we're not personally familiar with every person affiliated with or recommended by these two institutes, we cannot guarantee that a particular counselor they might recommend is reliable. You need to consult local clergy, mental health experts, and other nearby competent professionals before acting upon any referral. Make sure that any counselor you select is committed to keeping marriages together. Many counselors claim to be "neutral" on the issue of divorce, believing that individual fulfillment is more important than maintaining the marriage relationship.

[6] See Wallerstein, *et al.*, Chapter 3, "Growing Up Is Harder," is particularly helpful.

[7] David Popenoe and Barbara Dafoe Whitehead, *Should We Live Together? What Young Adults Need to Know About Cohabitation Before Marriage* (Brunswick, N. J.: The National Marriage Project, 1999), 2. See also online: http://marriage.rutgers.edu/publicat.htm

[8] David Popenoe and Barbara Dafoe Whitehead, *Sex Without Strings, Relationships Without Rings: Today's Young Singles Talk About Mating and Dating* (Brunswick, N. J.: The National Marriage Project, 2000), 7. See also online: http://marriage.rutgers.edu/publicat.htm.

[9] For an extensive list of problems associated with cohabiting, visit the "All About Cohabiting Before Marriage" Web site at http://hometown.aol.com/cohabiting/index.htm.

[10] Barbara Dafoe Whitehead, "How We Mate," *City Journal,* Summer 1999, 6. See also online: www.city-journal.org/.

[11] Michael J. McManus, *Marriage Savers: Helping Your Friends and Family Stay Married* (Grand Rapids, Mich.: Zondervan, 1993), 91.

[12] See Beth L. Bailey, *From Front Porch to Back Seat: Courtship in Twentieth-Century America* (Baltimore: Johns Hopkins University Press, 1988).

[13] McManus, 134-136. See also online: www.marriagesavers.org.

[14] *Family in America Report* (The Rockford Institute, 934 North Main Street, Rockford, Ill., 61103), February 1996, 4, reporting on a article by Barbara W. Sugland, "The Early Childhood HOME Inventory and HOME-Short Form in Differing Racial/Ethnic Groups" in the *Journal of Family Issues*, 16 (1995), 632–663.

[15] See St. John Chrysostom, "Homily V on Thessalonians," in vol. XIII of *The Nicene and Post-Nicene Fathers* (Grand Rapids, Mich.: Eerdmans, reprint May 1983). The works of St. John Chrysostom can also be accessed online at www.ccel.org/fathers2/NPNF1-09/TOC.htm. Translations slightly modified for modern usage.

[16] Michael P. Orsi, "A Case for Earlier Marriage," *Homiletic and Pastoral Review*, October 2001, 64-69.

[17] Neil Clark Warren, "Finding the Love of Your Life: How Not to Choose the Wrong Mate," *Focus on the Family Magazine*, November 1992, 2–3, and "Old Enough to Know: What is the Right Age to Get Married?" available online at www.eharmony.com/core/eharmony?cmd=ncw-articles&article=3.

[18] Robert Michael, *Determinants of Divorce in Sociological Economic.* Louis Levy-Garboua, ed. (Beverly Hills, Calif.: Sage Publications, 1979), 223–253.

[19] Michael, 233 and 236.

[20] Some good instruments to consider are Career Direct, The People Map, StrengthsFinder and StrengthsQuest, developed from a multimillion-dollar research effort by the Gallup Organization. All these instruments can be found through an online search.

[21] Contact The Rockford Institute at 934 North Main Street, Rockford, IL 61103; phone:(815) 964-5053; Web site: www.rockfordinstitute.org.

[22] Contact The Rockford Institute (see above).

[23] See *St. Joseph's Covenant Keepers Newsletter*, January 1999, Volume 5, Issue 1, 3.

[24] Pope John Paul II, "The Family and the Economy of the Future," an address given on March 8, 1996, published in *L'Osservatore Romano*, March 13, 1996.

[25] Lester C. Thurow, Professor of Economics at MIT, in "Changes in Capitalism Render One-Earner Families extinct," *USA Today*, January 27, 1997. See also Stephen Wood with James Burnham, *Christian Fatherhood*, 121–122.

[26] *Family in America Report*, February 1996, 2-3, reporting on a study by Jessie M. Tzeng of McGill University and Robert D. Mare of the University of Wisconsin-Madison, who interviewed 12,686 men and women, with annual follow-up interviews for eight years.

[27] For an explanation of the importance of tithing, see James Burnham and Stephen Wood, *Christian Fatherhood: The Eight Commitments of St. Joseph's Covenant Keepers* (Port Charlotte, Fla.: Family Life Center Publications, 1997), 116–119.

[28] A reliable way to know if you are ready to support a family is to work through the family budgeting and financial worksheets in Philip Lenahan, *Finances for Today's Catholic Families* (Temecula, Calif.: Financial Foundations for the Family, 1996).

[29] *Family in America Report,* February 1996, 2–3.

[30] *Catechism of the Catholic Church*, 2nd ed. (Vatican City: Libreria Editrice Vaticana, 1997), par. 1652, quoting *Gaudium et Spes,* 48.

[31] David H. Olson, John Defrain, and Amy K. Olson, *Building Relationships: Developing Skills for Life* (Minneapolis, Minn.: Life Innovations, 1999), 89–90. The chart of couple satisfaction is reproduced with the permission of David Olson.

[32] Olson *et al.*, 89-90.

[33] See Appendix I for a brief sample list of commitments. Also recommended for examples of "must have's" and "can't stands" in choosing a mate is Neil Clark Warren's, *Date . . . or Soul Mate? How to Know If Someone is Worth Pursuing in Two Dates or Less* (Nashville, Tenn.: Nelson, 2002). I do not agree with a few items included in Warren's lists, yet the book is invaluable when creating your written standards. See also Dr. Neil Clark Warren's online resources at www.eharmony.com.

[34] Michael, 244.

[35] *USA Today*, December 5, 2002, reporting on The American Religious Identification Survey (2001), the first national survey of divorce rates among same-faith and mixed-faith parents.

[36] Many of these couples have been inspired by Joshua Harris, *I Kissed Dating Goodbye* (Sisters, Or.: Multnomah, 1997).

[37] For a free online personality profile, go to www.eharmony.com. The wise *eharmony* plan for mate selection is to assist people in understanding themselves before choosing someone for a marriage partner.

[38] *Catechism,* par. 234.

[39] Quoted in the *Catechism,* par. 2365.

[40] Pope John Paul II, *The Role of the Christian Family in the Modern World (Familiaris Consortio)*, 25.

[41] Burnham and Wood, 153–154.

[42] Pope Pius XI, *On Christian Marriage (Casti Connubii)*, 41, 43, 111.

[43] *Journal of Marriage and Family*, 64 (February 2002), 180, reporting on a study by Catherine Cohan and Stacey Klienbaum, "Toward a Greater Understanding of the Cohabitation Effect: Premarital Cohabitation and Marital Communication," The Pennsylvania State University.

[44] www.prepinc.com.

[45] It is interesting to note that Isaac didn't see Rebekah's face until after they were married. In addition, Genesis 24:67 says that Isaac loved Rebekah *after* they were married. What a contrast to the pattern today, in which couples fall in love based upon appearances and then frequently fall out of love after marriage.

[46] The staff of the Family Life Center will pray with you for guidance in seeking a spouse and in your courtship, engagement, and new marriage. Click on prayer requests in the Contemporary Courtship section on the homepage of www.familylifecenter.net. You would also be wise to contact an orthodox religious order to pray for your needs.

[47] A letter written in 1808 and quoted in Ellen K. Rothman, *Hands and Hearts: A History of Courtship in America* (New York: Basic Books), 18.

[48] A Holy Hour is a Catholic devotional practice in the presence of the Blessed Sacrament that involves praying and reading Scripture for one hour, based upon Christ's challenge to "watch one hour" in Matthew 26:40 and Mark 14:37.

[49] Audiotape by Dr. Neil Clark Warren, *Hope: How Do I Keep My Hopes Up When I've Been So Devastatingly Unlucky–Or at Least Unsuccessful–at the Dating Game?* Tape 13 of audio series. Available from www.eharmony.com.

[50] The Family Life Center hopes to organize courtship conferences in the near future. Visit www.familylifecenter.net to see the latest conference schedule.

[51] Cardinal Alfonso Lopez Trujillo, *Preparation for the Sacrament of Marriage* (Vatican City: Pontifical Council for the Family, 1996), par. 35. This document mentions a fourth aspect to marital love: namely, that it is *fruitful*. For this fourth characteristic, see chapter 7.

[52] For a concise summary of the scriptural teachings on divorce and remarriage, see Burnham and Wood, *Christian Fatherhood*, 147–154.

[53] *Catechism*, par. 1646-1648.

[54] Janet E. Smith, *Humanae Vitae: A Generation Later* (Washington, D. C.: Catholic University of America Press, 1991), 127, 391. Among spouses teaching Natural Family Planning with the Couple to Couple League, the divorce rate is 1.4 percent. It is estimated that the divorce rate for all couples using Natural Family Planning may be up to three times this number, or 4.2 percent, which is still less than a tenth of the national divorce rate.

[55] *Catechism*, par. 2361, quoting *Familiaris Consortio*, 11.

[56] *Catechism*, par. 1643, quoting *Familiaris*, 13.

[57] *Catechism*, par. 2362, quoting *Gaudium et Spes*, 49, 2.

[58] *Catechism*, par. 2363 and 2366, quoting *Humanae Vitae*, 11–12.

[59] Charles D. Provan, *The Bible and Birth Control* (Monongahela, Penn.: Zimmer, 1989), 69–92.

[60] *Humanae Vitae*, 16.

[61] Contact the Couple to Couple League (www.ccli.org) headquartered in Cinncinnati, Ohio, for Natural Family Planning classes near you. The Family Life Office in your Catholic diocese will also be able to refer you to an NFP class.

[62] For a discussion of birth control and fatherhood, see Wood and Burnham, *Christian Fatherhood*, 125–139.

[63] Thinking about a vasectomy? Visit this site first! www.dontfixit.org. This Web site requires discernment, but nevertheless offers substantial help. Also see www.familylifecenter.net/txt/thegodsquad.html.

[64] For an excellent handbook to use in discovering both your vocation and your career, see Rick Sarkisian, *LifeWork: Finding Your Purpose in Life* (San Francisco: Ignatius, 1997).

[65] For a treatment of time demands upon fathers, see Burnham and Wood, *Christian Fatherhood*, 74–84.

[66] Michael D. O'Brien, *A Landscape with Dragons: The Battle for Your Child's Mind* (San Francisco: Ignatius, 1998), 164.

[67] Anderson Spickard, M.D., and Barbara R. Thompson, *Dying for a Drink: What You Should Know About Alcoholism* (Waco, Tex.: Word, 1985), 194–195. Unfortunately, this excellent book is out of print. With Dr. Spickard's permission, we have posted his two-page letter at www.familylifecenter.net.

[68] Spickard, 194.

[69] See the *Catechism*, 1809.

[70] See Warren, *Date*. I do not endorse all his suggested items.

[71] James Prochaska, John Norcross, and Carlo Diclemente, *Changing for Good* (New York: Quill, 2002).

[72] This same process will double your chances of quitting smoking, changing to a healthier diet, losing weight, starting an exercise program, acquiring a virtue, or accomplishing some task you've tried without success to complete.

Bibliography

Helpful Catholic resources

Carol, Angela. *St. Raphael.* Rockford, Ill.: TAN, 1999.

Catechism of the Catholic Church, 2nd ed. Vatican City: Libreria Editrice Vaticana, 1997. See especially paragraphs 1601, 1666, 2331–2400.

Doyle, Charles Hugo. *Blame No One But Yourself: Marriage Counsels to Teen-Agers and All Those Contemplating Wedlock.* Tarrytown, New York: Nugent, 1955.

Elliott, Msgr. Peter. *What God Has Joined: The Sacramentality of Marriage.* New York: Alba House, 1990.

Healy, Edwin F., S.J. *Teacher's Manual for Marriage Guidance.* Chicago: Loyola University, 1949.

Kippley, John. *Marriage Is for Keeps: Foundations for Christian Marriage.* Cincinnati: Foundation for the Family, 1994.

Marks, Frederick W. *A Catholic Handbook for Engaged and Newly Married Couples.* Milford, Ohio: The Riehle Foundation, 1994.

National Conference of Catholic Bishops, Committee for Pastoral Research and Practices. *Faithful to Each Other Forever: A Catholic Handbook of Pastoral Help for Marriage Preparation.* Washington, D.C.: United States Catholic Conference, Office of Publishing and Promotion Services, 1989.

O'Brien, Fr. John A. *Courtship and Marriage: Happiness in the Home.* Patterson, N. J.: St. Anthony Guild, 1949.

Sheen, Archbishop Fulton J. *Three to Get Married.* Princeton: Scepter, 1951.

Trujillo, Cardinal Alfonso Lopez. *Preparation for the Sacrament of Marriage*. Vatican City: Pontifical Council for the Family, 1996.

von Hildebrand, Dietrich. *Marriage: The Mystery of Faithful Love*. Manchester, N. H.: Sophia Institute, 1991.

Papal documents on marriage and family life

All papal documents listed are available for free download from www.dads.org and www.familylifecenter.net.

* Leo XIII, *On Christian Marriage* [*Arcanum Divinae*], 1880.

* Pius XI, *On Christian Marriage* [*Casti Connubii*], 1930.

* Paul VI, *Of Human Life* [*Humanae Vitae*], 1968.

* John Paul II, *The Role of the Christian Family in the Modern World* [*Familiaris Consortio*], 1981.

* John Paul II, *Letter to Families*, 1994.

Other Worthwhile Readings

A listing here does not mean an unqualified endorsement.

Bailey, Beth L. *From Front Porch to Back Seat: Courtship in Twentieth-Century America.* Baltimore: Johns Hopkins University, 1988.

Blankenhorn, David. *Fatherless America.* New York: Basic, 1995.

Dufoyer, Pierre. *Marriage: A Word to Young Men.* New York: P. J. Kennedy & Sons, 1963.

Eberly, Don E., ed. *The Faith Factor in Fatherhood.* Lanham, Md.: Lexington, 1999.

Gallagher, Maggie. *Enemies of Eros: How the Sexual Revolution Is Killing Family, Marriage, and Sex and What We Can Do About It.* Chicago: Bonus, 1989.

Gallagher, Maggie, and Linda J. Waite. *The Case for Marriage: Why Married People Are Happier, Healthier, and Better Off Financially.* New York: Doubleday, 2000.

Gottman, John. *Why Marriages Succeed or Fail . . . And How You Can Make Yours Last.* New York: Simon & Schuster, 1994.

Harris, Joshua. *I Kissed Dating Goodbye.* Sisters, Or.: Multnomah, 1997.

Horn, Wade F., David Blankenhorn, and Mitchell B. Pearlstein, eds. *The Fatherhood Movement: A Call to Action.* Lanham, Maryland: Lexington, 1999.

Kass, Amy A. and Leon R. Kass, eds. *Wing to Wing, Oar to Oar: Readings on Courting and Marrying.* Notre Dame, Indiana: University of Notre Dame, 2000.

Mason, Mike. *The Mystery of Marriage: As Iron Sharpens Iron.* Portland, Oregon: Multnomah, 1985.

McManus, Michael J. *Marriage Savers: Helping Your Friends and Family Avoid Divorce.* Grand Rapids, Michigan: Zondervan, 1995.

Olson, David H., John DeFrain, and Amy K. Olson. *Building Relationships: Developing Skills for Life.* Minneapolis: Life Innovations, 1999.

Popenoe, David, and Barbara Dafoe Whitehead. *The State of Our Unions 2000: The Social Health of Marriage in America.* New Brunswick, New Jersey: The National Marriage Project, Rutgers University, 2000. Available online at www.marriage.rutgers.edu/publicat.htm.

Popenoe, David, and Barbara Dafoe Whitehead. "Should We Live Together? What Young Adults Need to Know About Cohabitation Before Marriage." New Brunswick, N. J.: The National Marriage Project, Rutgers University, 1999. Available online at www.marriage.rutgers.edu/publicat.htm.

Rothman, Ellen K. *Hands and Hearts: A History of Courtship in America.* New York: Basic Books, 1984.

Sollee, Diane. *Coalition for Marriage, Family, and Couples Education (CMFCE).* An abundant collection of articles and resources for marriage and family life are posted on this helpful Web site. Go to www.smartmarriages.com.

Voth, Harold M. *Families: The Future of America.* Chicago: Regnery Gateway, 1984.

Wallerstein, Judith S., Julia M. Lewis, Sandra Blakeslee. *The Unexpected Legacy of Divorce: A 25-Year Landmark Study.* New York: Hyperion, 2000.

Warren, Neil Clark. *Date . . . Or Soul Mate? How to Know If Someone Is Worth Pursuing in Two Dates or Less.* Nashville: Thomas Nelson, 2002.

Wright, H. Norman. *Premarital Counseling.* Chicago: Moody, 1977.

Resources

For any of the resources below visit www.familylifecenter.net or www.dads.org. You can also call (800) 705-6131.

Stuff Just for Men from St. Joseph's Covenant Keepers

Most men make the mistake of waiting until their first child arrives to learn the skills of fatherhood. Start learning about fatherhood *now*. The earlier you begin preparing for fatherhood, the more effective father you'll be. Check out these resources:

- **www.dads.org** is a Web site loaded with free materials for Christian husbands and fathers.

- *Christian Fatherhood: The Eight Commitments of St. Joseph's Covenant Keepers* by Stephen Wood with James Burnham. A great book with practical tools to prepare you for one of the greatest challenges any man can have —being a great Christian father.

- *St. Joseph's Covenant Keepers Newsletter,* a free e-newsletter. Subscribe at **www.dads.org**.

Contemporary Courtship

www.familylifecenter.net, the Family Life Center's companion Web site to **www.dads.org**, has a special Contemporary Courtship section for young men and women. You'll find courtship news, articles, free online talks, resources, and links to recommended sites.

Catalog

The Family Life Center offers a *free* catalog of a wide selection of tapes, books, and videos on courtship, marriage, faith, family life, and fatherhood. You can also order all items in our online catalog at www.dads.org, or at www.familylifecenter.net.

Conferences

The Family Life Center holds conferences throughout North America. For a *free* list of upcoming conferences, visit either of our Web sites. The Family Life Center also sponsors and participates in conferences for couples on marriage, parenting, homeschooling, faith, and family life. To bring a conference to your community, call us for an information pack.

For Women You Know

The ABCs of Choosing a Good Husband by Stephen Wood. This companion to the book you have just read is a treasure filled with wisdom and practical advice for women on how to find and marry the man of their dreams. This bestseller is available both in print and as an audio book-on-tape.

Extra copies

Order online for discount prices on extra copies of either of the *ABCs* books for your friends, family members, small group, or parish. Go to www.dads.org or www.familylifecenter.net. Or call toll-free number, (800) 705-6131 (between 9 A.M. and 5 P.M. EST), or contact us at:

Family Life Center
22226 Westchester Boulevard
Port Charlotte, FL 33952
Phone: (941) 764-8565; Fax: (941) 743-5352;
e-mail: mail@familylifecenter.net

About the Author

Steve Wood has led youth, campus, and pro-life ministries. A graduate of Gordon-Conwell Theological Seminary, he served as an Evangelical pastor for a decade before starting the Family Life Center International in 1992.

He is also the founder of St. Joseph's Covenant Keepers, a movement that seeks to transform society through the transformation of fathers and families. Utilizing his book *Christian Fatherhood*, audio and video tapes, television, radio and conferences, Steve has reached tens of thousands of men in the USA, Canada and overseas with a message of Christian faith and responsibility. He is the host of the live *Faith and Family* broadcasts on EWTN worldwide radio (www.ewtn.com), as well as the host of *The Carpenter Shop*, a show for fathers on EWTN worldwide television.

A member of the American Counseling Association, Steve is also a Certified Family Life Educator. In addition, he is a professional Christian Life Coach with a private practice (www.halftimecoaching.com) offering special coaching services for those seeking a life partner.

Steve and Karen Wood have been married twenty-five years and are the parents of eight children.